What the Mass Means

What the Mass Means

An Introduction to the Rites of the Latin Mass

FR. VICTOR J. HINTGEN

TAN BOOKS
GASTONIA, NORTH CAROLINA

Nihil Obstat: Anthony Kreimer, PhD
Censor Librorum

Imprimatur: Francis J. L. Beckman, STD
Archbishop of Dubuque
Dubuque October 24 1936
Feast of St. Raphael

Originally published in 1936 as *What the Mass Means: An Explanation of the Prayers and Ceremonies of the Holy Sacrifice* by Our Sunday Visitor Press.

Cover design by David Ferris—www.davidferrisdesign.com

ISBN: 978-1-5051-2896-3
Kindle ISBN: 978-1-5051-2897-0
ePUB ISBN: 978-1-5051-2898-7

Published in the United States by
TAN Books
PO Box 269
Gastonia, NC 28053
www.TANBooks.com

Printed in the United States of America

"Our Lady of the Most Blessed Sacrament,
Mother and Model of Adorers,
pray for us who have recourse to thee."

"Hear, O Lord Jesus Christ, the prayers of Thy servants and have mercy on us: who with the Father and Holy Ghost lives and reigns forever and ever. Amen."

Contents

Introduction 1

Preparation 5

Prayers at the Foot of the Altar 5

The Confiteor 7

The Introit 12

The Kyrie Eleison 14

The Gloria in Excelsis 15

Instruction 17

The Dominus Vobiscum 17

The Collects 19

Epistle 24

Gradual and Alleluia, Tract, and Sequence 25

The Gospel 28

The Credo 35

Offertory 37

Offertory Prayers 37

The Lavabo 51

The Orate Fratres 54

The Secret 58

The Consecration 61

The Preface and Sanctus 61

Canon 66

Communion 93

The Our Father 93

The Breaking of the Host 101

The Agnus Dei 103

Prayer of Peace .106
Prayers before Communion .109
The Communion .111
After the Communion .115
The Communion Verse and Postcommunion Prayer.116
The Blessing and Dismissal .118
The Last Gospel .120
Summary 123
A Review of Sacrifice .123
A Review of the Offertory .124
A Review of the Consecration .126
A Review of the Communion.128
An Exhortation .131

Introduction

Greatest Act of Worship

The Mass is our greatest act of worship. It is our sacrifice. Its importance comes from the fact that it is a renewal and a continuation of the Sacrifice of Christ on the Cross on the hill of Calvary. We have heard many times that the Mass is our most influential prayer; that it is a most abundant source of benefit to both the living and the dead. In the Mass, we adore the Highest Lord and also make atonement for having offended Him through sin.

We are certainly interested in this highest act of Religion! It means so much to us. To help us to understand and appreciate the Mass, the Church has wisely ornamented it with what we call ceremonies and symbols. These are various actions, gestures and movements which tell a story. How often we have heard the expression, "actions speak louder than words"! Everything we see and hear during the Divine Sacrifice means something and is a key part in telling the story of a reality that transcends all things human.

The Mass, an Educator

In teaching children, and even adults, the good teacher frequently tells stories and draws pictures and illustrations and diagrams. The listeners are better able to understand when the teacher uses this method. The Church uses the picture method, or the black-board method when it uses ceremonies and symbols. You remember in St. Mark's gospel (7:34) the story of Our Lord's miraculous cure of one deaf and dumb. "And He [Christ] put his fingers into His ears, and spitting, he touched his tongue: and looking up to heaven he groaned, and said to him: *Ephpheta,* which is, Be thou opened." We know the Savior could just as easily have cured this unfortunate one had He not used all this ceremonial in the action. But Jesus used this round-about way to teach a lesson through the groan, the spittle, the touching of the tongue. So does the Church teach in its use of all these externals in the Mass.

These signs and actions also help us to pray better. Is it not easier to pray when we strike our breast, or when we kneel, or when we bow? These actions also express our deep and fervent sorrow and littleness. We know pictures and statues help us keep our easily-distracted mind fixed on religious ideas. Man is made up not only of body and senses but also of soul and spirit. The body with its senses helps the soul and mind pray and worship better. Man needs signs and symbols and ceremonies to impress him; to touch his heart; to fix his wandering thoughts—to teach him.

Speaking of the impressive ceremonies of the Mass, the Council of Trent declares, "Since by reason of his nature man is so constituted that without exterior aid he can not easily rise to the contemplation of divine things, the Church, as a devoted mother, has therefore introduced into her liturgy certain usages, as, for example, that some portions of the Mass should be recited in a low tone, others in a loud tone of voice. In like manner, certain ceremonies, for instance the blessings, the use of lights, incense, vestments and many things of that nature, she employs by Apostolic custom and tradition, in order both to manifest thereby the majesty of the great sacrifice, as well as to animate the minds of the faithful by these visible signs of religion and piety, to the consideration of the sublime mysteries hidden within this sacrifice" (Sess. 22, c. 5.).

The diamond is a beautiful gem. In order to bring out its beauty, a jeweler mounts it in a pin, or a ring. The ceremonies and prayers of the Mass, we may say, are like the mounting and setting to the diamond—they bring out the beauty of the Sacrifice. Sacrifice, since it is the highest act in religion, is most beautiful in itself. In order that we may understand and appreciate this beauty, it is given to us mounted in a gorgeous ceremonial.

Father Faber, a convert and one who has written well on the Blessed Sacrament, writes, "[The Mass] is the most beautiful thing this side of heaven . . . it came forth out of the grand mind of the Church and lifted us out of earth and out of self."

Questions for Discussion

1. Why is the Mass our greatest act of worship?
2. What is a sacrifice? What is worship?
3. What is meant by adoration? By atonement?
4. Explain the purpose and use of ceremonies.
5. Name some ceremonies and symbols.

Preparation

Prayers at the Foot of the Altar

Having arranged the chalice for Mass and opened the Missal, the priest descends to the foot of the altar. There he makes the Sign of the Cross with the usual words. It is certainly fitting and wise that the priest and people should begin this Sacrifice with the Sign of the Cross; for the Mass is Christ's redeeming death on the cross continued and re-presented. The Mass brings us back to the cross on Calvary. The Sign of the Cross is also a synopsis, a summary of our faith. We begin the Mass with a short act of faith in the Trinity and in the Redemption.

Written in Exile

There follows the 42nd Psalm. This inspired poem was written by King David when he was in exile, fleeing from his rebellious son, Absolom. The antiphon is said first, "I will go unto the altar of God. Unto God Who giveth joy to my youth." The antiphon strikes the key-note of the psalm; it gives the main idea of the poem.

David is in exile. He regrets immensely he is not able to go to the temple and take part in the worship. He longs and yearns to pray and sacrifice in Jerusalem. He begs God to be his judge—a just judge. God knows David is innocent; that his enemies led by the ungrateful Absolom, judge him wrongly. David feels God allows this present revolt as a punishment for his sins. He begs God to send him help, light and truth, that he may bear his misery humbly. The exiled king hopes in his Creator and promises on his return to the holy city of Jerusalem, to sing the praises of the Lord to the accompaniment of his harp. In the temple he will find joy and gladness. When he offers his sacrifice at the altar, his heart will bound with the joy which was his in youth when he knew no sorrow.

Beautiful Preparation

Isn't this a beautiful preparation for our Mass? We repeat with the priest this psalm of David. We beg God humbly and contritely to hear our prayers in our extreme need. We, like David, are exiles in this valley of tears. We are troubled with enemies of soul and body. We need strength and light and truth so very badly. God will judge us and we beg Him to be favorable to us. He knows how hard we try to serve Him. Our present sorrows will pass; He will dry the tears from our eyes. We are anxious to offer Him this sacrifice of the Mass. We are happy that we can obtain forgiveness and help at the altar. Our sadness over our helplessness and loneliness turns to thrilling joy as we anticipate the wealth of this Sacrifice of the Mass. Herein we find joy, the only real, lasting and true joy—the joy of youth, the joy of a spiritual new life, in the grace and friendship of God.

Then is said the "Glory be to the Father, etc." We close this matchless prayer-psalm with a gladsome cry of praise and thanks to each person of the Trinity. During the prayer we bow, to express our reverence and humility before the triune God.

Omitted at Requiems

Since this 42nd psalm and the "Glory be to the Father" are joyful prayers, they are omitted at Requiem Masses and Masses of Passion-week. At these Masses we are expected to be mourning for the departed and for the suffering Savior.

Questions for Discussion

1. Why do we begin the Mass with a Sign of the Cross?
2. Can you make this sign correctly?
3. Who was King David? What is a psalm? An antiphon? (Consult the Catholic Encyclopedia or a good dictionary).
4. Give the meaning of Psalm 42 verse by verse. (To be found in the Old Testament).
5. Why is this psalm such a beautiful preparation for Mass?

THE CONFITEOR

Realizing that only he who is "innocent in hands, and clean of heart" may "go up to the mountain of the Lord, and stand in His holy place" (Psalm 23:3), the priest makes a public acknowledgment of his transgressions in the *Confiteor*. Before this general confession, he blesses himself with the strengthening words, "Our help is in the name of the Lord, who made heaven and earth." The priest fears, as it were, to begin this august mystery of the Mass in which he is to speak for Christ. Appreciating somewhat his responsibility, he asks God for help and strength. To call on the name of one, means to call on that person; "name" means person, individual. He makes the Sign of the Cross, for through the cross we have the saving help of the Savior. "I have lifted up my eyes to the mountains, from whence help shall come to me" (Psalm 120:1).

Then follows the *Confiteor* which means, "I confess." The priest confesses first to Almighty God whom we have offended above all. Then, we confess our guilt to the Blessed Virgin. We have not directly offended her, but by offending the Son, we have also indirectly offended her. Well may we be ashamed before her who shared not our offenses yet suffered because of them in the passion of her Son.

Then Michael, the Archangel, is mentioned. Michael is the valiant and faithful angel warrior who hurled the rebellious angels into hell. To him we confess—to him who is tried and true. Certainly, we have failed where he remained loyal and steadfast. Next, an acknowledgment of sin is made to St. John the Baptist, the precursor of the Lord in the preaching of penance for the remission of sins. Then comes "the holy apostles Peter and Paul and all the saints." All these have overcome the temptations to which we have surrendered; they have been victorious through the Blood of the Lamb of God—that life-giving Blood which we, in our sins, have thrown back to Heaven in refusal. By our sins, we have grieved all these saints; we have offended and insulted them by our wrong-doings, for we cast aside that for which they died.

We confess our guilt also to all the living, "to you brethren." Through this confession we wish to repair our bad example, we wish to correct the scandal we have caused. Sin is the greatest social evil. Sin begets sin; sin creates disharmony. Then striking his breast, the priest sadly says, "Through my fault, through my fault, through my most grevious fault." In this action is eloquent symbolism—the striking of the breast expresses deep regret, for the heart was considered as a cause of undue affection for sin and so deserves to be chastised and blamed. The three-fold striking expresses symbolically the intense, the very sincere regret and contrition. The deep inclination of the body and the eyes cast to earth and the hands folded all dramatically bespeak the guilty priest's misery and shame before the good and forgiving Lord. There is the minister before the altar as an ungrateful servant, his back loaded with heavy offenses, his hands tied as God's runaway prisoner, his eyes cast to the floor as one guilty and ashamed to face the truth.

The *Confiteor* recalls the sixteenth stanza of the *Dies Irae* said at Requiems, "Kneeling and prostrate I pray, with a heart contrite as though crushed to ashes; care Thou for me at my last hour." "A sacrifice to God is an afflicted spirit. A contrite and humble heart, O God, thou wilt not despise" (Psalm 50).

There follows now the second part of the *Confiteor*, or the public confession of sins in general. Now we beg the saints invoked in the first half to pray for us. We pray the Blessed Virgin, the Mother of divine grace, the Mother of mercy, the refuge of sinners, our life, our sweetness and our hope, to win God's forgiveness for us. We likewise beg Saint Michael, our safeguard against the devil, to obtain mercy for us; we beg St. John the Baptist, saints Peter and Paul and all the saints to ask the Lord God for us. We ask the friends of the King to obtain for us miserable traitors, His mercy and forgiveness. Humbly, we beg the people assembled to pray also for us, that we may in a worthy and becoming manner celebrate this Mystery.

The people, now through the altar boy, make their public avowal of sin, using the words which the priest used with one exception. Where the priest said, "You brethren," the people say, "You, Father."

It is hardly necessary to mention the value of the *Confiteor*. This should be now evident to all who considered it seriously as a preparation for Mass. And still, how often the people neglect either to say it, or to say it humbly and contritely? The altar-boys say it aloud for the congregation and the congregation should say it privately with great compunction of heart, bowing and striking their breasts. The *Confiteor* is a sacramental, and, as you know, sacramentals remit venial sins on account of the sorrow, love, faith, good resolutions, and other good thoughts, words, deeds, and desires which they arouse and evoke.

The people and priest pray for each other in the words:

"May the Almighty God have mercy upon you, and bring you to life everlasting."

Then the priest, making the Sign of the Cross, says an absolving prayer. (This is not the absolution given in Penance):

"May the Almighty and most Merciful Lord grant us pardon, ✠ absolution and remission of our sins."

The priest and the altar-boys, as spokesmen for the congregation, recite three short ejaculations begging mercy and help.

Ascending the altar, the priest prays that "We may be worthy to enter with pure minds into the Holy of Holies."

In the Mass, the priest represents "the high priest, Jesus Christ, holy, innocent, undefiled, separated from sinners, and made higher than the heavens" (Hebrews 7:26). No wonder he asks so often that the Father above, remit his past offenses and transgressions; no wonder he prays that he may be less unworthy to offer this Sacrifice for the world!

"Who shall ascend into the mountain of the Lord: or who shall stand in his holy place? The innocent of hands and clean of heart" (Psalm 23).

These sentiments of sorrow and amendment of life are also expressed in the prayer said at the altar:

"We beseech Thee, O Lord, by the merits of Thy saints [here, he kisses the altar] whose relics are here, and of all the saints, that Thou wouldst vouchsafe to forgive me all my sins. Amen."

The priest kisses the altar in reverence and respect to all the saints, especially those whose relics are in the altar stone. The altar represents Christ Himself, in whom and through whom alone we can present to God acceptable sacrifices and prayers. In the center of the altar, where the chalice rests, is a small sealed cavity enclosing the relics of some martyrs. Every altar has this altar stone with relics for the reason that the first Christians during the persecutions said Mass in the Catacombs, using the tombs of the martyrs as altars. There is also the reason of fitness: they who shed their blood for Christ should rest in the altar, whereon is celebrated the Sacrifice of the Master who gave them the strengthening grace of martyrdom. They died for Christ and it is appropriate that they rest in the altar whereon His death is represented. Saint John, in his vision, "saw under the altar the souls of them that were slain for the word of God and for the testimony which they held" (Apocalypse 6:9).

Questions for Discussion

1. What does *Confiteor* mean? Why is it said at this time?
2. Why do we confess to the Blessed Virgin? To the apostles? To our brethren?
3. Why do we strike our breasts during this prayer?
4. Does the *Confiteor* remove sin? Is it like confession?
5. Why does the priest kiss the altar when he ascends to the altar?
6. Why are relics in the altar-stone?

THE INTROIT

The *Introit* (which is Latin for "he enters") of our Mass is a remnant of the complete psalm which was sung in its entirety, while the celebrant and his assisting ministers proceeded from the secretorium (our sacristy) to the foot of the altar. In the first centuries, up to the Avignon residence of the Popes, the entry of the clergy from the front of the church formed a solemn and stately procession. The Masses then, at least the public ones, were sung Masses. Now, due to changed conditions, we no longer have the old entrance processions with the singing of a complete psalm. The priest, and the choir at High Mass, now say the antiphon, one verse of a psalm and the *Glory be to the Father* at the epistle side of the altar.

The celebrant at the first word of the *Introit* blesses himself with the Sign of the Cross. This practice goes back to the time when the *Introit* was the actual beginning of the Mass and the prayers of preparation at the foot of the altar were not ordered. At a Requiem Mass, the priest does not sign himself, but traces a cross over the Mass-book. This cross is not for the Missal, but for the departed souls who are the special concern of the Church during this Mass. Nor is the *Glory be to the Father* said at the *Introit* of Requiems and the penitential Masses, for during these Masses the Church expresses no indication of joy and gladness.

The *Introit* is a variable portion of the Mass, that is, it changes with the different Masses. It is usually of striking beauty and has special reference to the day or to the saint whose feast is commemorated; it expresses briefly the prevailing idea in that particular Mass. Cardinal Wiseman says beautifully of the *Introit*, "It seems intended to be the keynote to the whole service; which being one in its essence, yet adapts itself to all our wants, whether of propitiation or of thanksgiving; whether of evils to be averted or of blessings to be gained. Sometimes this introductory verse is loud and joyous,—'Let us rejoice in the Lord'; sometimes low and plaintive,—'Lord, have mercy on me'; in the Paschal solemnity the *Alleluia* rings through it all, like a peal of cheerful bells; in Passion-tide, even the *Glory be to the Father* is silent, and it falls melancholy and dull; when a saint is commemorated, the nature of his virtues and triumphs is at once proclaimed; if it be a festival of Our Lord, the mystery which it celebrates is solemnly announced."

Let us give a few examples to illustrate the idea of the *Introit*. For the third Mass on Christmas, it begins: "A Child has been born to us and a Son has been given us." The first line of Easter Sunday proclaims: "I am risen and I am still with thee, Alleluia, etc." At the Requiem Mass: "Eternal rest give them, O Lord, and let perpetual light shine upon them."

Since the Mass directly began with the *Introit* for many centuries, its first words were used to designate the Mass of the day. So even today we still call the third Sunday in Advent, *Gaudete* Sunday, the fourth Sunday in Lent, *Laetare* Sunday, the first Sunday after Easter, *Quasi modo* Sunday, and the Masses "in black," *Requiem* Masses.

Questions for Discussion

1. What is the history of the *Introit*?
2. What is its purpose or spirit?
3. What changes take place in the *Introit* and in the *Confiteor* at a Requiem Mass, and why do they occur?

THE KYRIE ELEISON

The *Kyrie Eleison* and the *Christe Eleison* are Greek expressions meaning "Lord, have mercy on us! Christ, have mercy on us!" The nine "*Kyries*" and "*Christes*" are all that remain of a litany of such invocations which were originally sung at this part of the Mass by the clergy and the people, or by the choirs.

This prayer is a cry for mercy and help, which the Church addresses to the Three Persons of the Blessed Trinity; three to the Father, three to the Son and three to the Holy Ghost. The *Kyrie Eleison* is a short but powerful prayer. Short prayers ever seem to be the most sincere and truthful. When a heart is overflowing with sentiments, it gives expression to its emotions in short, meaningful words. There is no need, no time to use long sentences for the listener attends more to the sincerity of the petitioner than to his language. The *Kyrie* and the *Christe* are repeated several times to tell the extreme want and earnest desire of the one imploring aid.

The persistent cry for mercy and forgiveness and assistance in the *Kyrie* reminds one of this line from the Gospel: "Yet if he shall continue knocking, I say to you although he will not rise and give him, because he is his friend; yet, because of his importunity, he will rise and give him as many as he needeth" (Luke 11:8). It also reminds one of the humble prayer of the blind man of Jericho: "Jesus, son of David, have mercy on me!" (Luke 18:35). And again, of the piteous petition of the ten lepers, "Lord have mercy on us!" (Luke 17:12).

The Kyrie was never translated from its Greek into Latin, the reason being, most likely, that there was no need, for its meaning was well known to the Latins, so perfectly human a prayer it was.

Questions for Discussion

1. What is the meaning and spirit of the *Kyrie Eleison?*
2. Why is this Greek prayer in a Latin Mass?

THE GLORIA IN EXCELSIS

After humbly and contritely beseeching the Three Persons in one God to have mercy on us, we naturally feel happy over the Lord's certain merciful answer; we anticipate in great gladness of heart His blotting out of our misdeeds. Therefore, with a joyful heart and loud voice we sing the *Gloria*, "Glory to God in the highest, and peace on earth to men of good-will." Since the *Gloria* is a hymn of joy, it also is omitted at Masses of Requiem and penitential Masses.

Sacrifice, the supreme act of worship, has four ends: the adoration of God for His glory, giving thanks to God for goods received, petitioning God for help, and making reparation or satisfaction for sins committed against God. That is, worship is either an act of adoration, thanksgiving, petition, or satisfaction. The Mass is the perfect sacrifice of adoration, of thanksgiving, of petition, and of satisfaction for sin, and within the Mass how well are the four ends of the Sacrifice expressed in the *Gloria!* The text itself goes through them—we praise Him; we adore Him; we bless Him, that is, we proclaim we recognize His blessings; we glorify Him, that is, give Him honor and glory through good living and worship; we pray for mercy for the sins we have committed; we give Him thanks for having sent His Son, Jesus Christ, to redeem us. Christ is the glory of God; He is the incarnate grandeur and majesty of God. "All have sinned and do need the glory of God," that is, the Son of God (Romans 3:25). Again, we call on the Son, "the

Lamb of God who taketh away the sins of the world," to have mercy on us. How the Church wishes us to realize that there is little fruit for us in the Mass unless we have a contrite heart! The best preparation for Mass is our gift of a generous and clean heart. A sacrifice to God is an afflicted spirit. "A contrite and humble heart, O God, Thou wilt not despise" (Psalm 50). The *Gloria* tells us of a necessary reason for our attendance at Mass: to give glory to God as our Lord and Savior did by His life, and to obtain needy peace, that peace which the Prince of Peace alone can give (John 16:33; 14:27).

With thrilling joy and rapid hearts, may we sing or pray the *Gloria,* with the zest and alacrity of the angels on Christmas. "Singing and making melody in your hearts to the Lord" (Ephesians 5:19). "Let us be glad and rejoice and give glory to Him, the Lord our God, the Almighty" (Apocalypse 19:16).

Questions for Discussion

1. What are the ends of sacrifice? How do these fit well with the Mass?
2. How does the *Gloria in Excelsis* fit in the Mass?
3. What is meant by glory? By peace?
4. Read in St. Luke the account of Our Lord's birth and the angels' welcome (Luke 2).
5. Explain phrase by phrase the different aspects of worship expressed in the *Gloria in Excelsis?*

Instruction

The Dominus Vobiscum

At the conclusion of the *Gloria,* after the celebrant has made the Sign of the Cross on himself, he kisses the altar near the altar-stone and then greets the people with the words *Dominus Vobiscum, "The Lord be with you!"* Kissing the altar is a sign of reverence and love. The altar represents Christ Himself, who is for us priest, victim and altar. Christ is indeed the living Cornerstone, upon whom rests the Church. Several Scripture passages attest to this: "Jesus Christ Himself being the chief cornerstone" (Ephesians 2:20); "The stone which the builders rejected, the same is become the head of the corner" (Matt. 21:42); "A living stone, rejected indeed by men but chosen and made honorable by God" (1 Peter 2:4).

In kissing the altar, the priest expresses his love and devotion not only for Christ but also for the martyrs, the saints in heaven: the Church Triumphant. We have already mentioned that in the altar-stone are the relics of saints. What is more correct than to rest the Body and Blood of the Redeemer upon the hallowed remains of those saintly servants who lived and died for Him and who were sanctified through His Flesh and Blood, who imitated their Savior in giving their lives in testimony to the Truth!

The priest, having kissed the altar, turns and faces the congregation, extends and joins his hands and salutes them with the affectionate words, "The Lord be with you"! What better blessing could the priest wish for his people than that the Lord be with them; for if God be with us, who can be against us (Romans 8:31)? What greater blessing than "The Lord be with you!" can anyone wish upon another? This is the very wish which St. Paul frequently sent his friends. In kissing the altar before greeting the people, the celebrant not only expresses his faith in Christ and the Church but also wishes to indicate that the best gifts in life come from God through the altar. If we wish to live a Christ-like life, we must keep close to the altar.

In greeting his people, the celebrant extends his arms and then rejoins them. This gesture tells of the priest's intense prayer for the people; he is begging Heaven to grant his wish and to give it abundantly, over-flowing, and the people wish the same to him. The response to *Dominus vobiscum* by the people is, *Et cum spiritu tuo,* "And with thy spirit," meaning, "may the Lord be with you also, father."

These eight instances of *Dominus Vobiscum* in the Mass show how closely in spirit and in action the celebrant and the congregation should be at Mass. Both are performing the august Sacrifice, both, like Moses, are on holy ground, and both desperately need the helping prayer of the other. The shepherd prays for his flock, while the flock prays for its shepherd, so that each may in a worthy and becoming manner offer this holy Sacrifice to the Most High. Seeing what this all means, the people should return their greeting of "And with you also" in a sincere way. It is only polite and respectable that the people return with affection the priest's tender greeting. Oftentimes, only the altar-boy responds aloud for the congregation, yet the congregation ought to answer in their hearts this heartfelt wish: "may the Lord be with you also, father."

Eight times during the Mass does the priest wish the special presence of the Lord with His people. Before the orations (also known as collects or prayers), he asks for them His assistance that they pray well. Before the Gospel, the priest asks the Lord to grant them the understanding and love of the Gospel truths. Before the Offertory, the priest asks that they be generous in their offering, not necessarily of the coin but especially the gift of one's self. At the Preface, the *Dominus Vobiscum* expresses the celebrant's wish that the people express their adoration and thanks well; and at the Communion that they prepare fervently for His coming either sacramentally or spiritually. Then at the Post-Communion prayers that the people keep their Guest always with them by remaining in grace; and for the last time at the close of Mass, that they appreciate the blessing and abiding presence of their Friend and Savior.

Questions for Discussion

1. Why does the priest kiss the altar now?
2. What is the meaning of this greeting? Should the people answer the priest's greeting? Why?
3. Why does the priest extend his hands?
4. How often, and when, does the celebrant use this greeting?

THE COLLECTS

The celebrant now goes to the epistle side of the altar to pray the *Collects*, or what are often named the *Orations* or *Prayers* of the Mass. Most likely, this prayer is called the *Collects* from the fact that originally it was a prayer which was said when the faithful had assembled at an appointed place, or church, whence they walked in procession to the Station-Church where the Pope said Mass.

After the first three centuries, at certain times, the Pope himself would say the Mass in some particular church designated beforehand. This church was called then the Station. We still have this direction in the Missal for various Masses through the year. This has been preserved most often in penitential seasons, such as the Masses of Advent, Ember Days, or Lent, e. g., Station at St. Paul.

At the gathering of the people and, probably, also on their arrival at the Station, a prayer, the *Collect,* was said. *Collect* is from the Latin, "Colligere," meaning to "gather," to "assemble." When after many centuries these station-Masses with their preliminary processions were not possible, the *Collect* and what remains of a long litany, the *Kyrie Eleison,* were said, as they are now, at the first part of every Mass.

At the beginning of the prayer or oration, the priest turns toward the crucifix, making a slight bow, and says, "Oremus" (in English, "let us pray"). He turns toward the crucifix as a greeting to the Savior, in recognition of His help which alone saves. This gesture expresses also our intention to pray in His name as He suggested (John 14:13). During the prayer, the priest has his hands extended the height and width of the shoulders. This method of praying expresses the earnestness and the sincerity of the petitioner. When we want things very urgently do we not beg with outstretched arms? When a child wants to be taken up by his mother, does he not plead with outstretched hands? The priest at the altar prays in similar fashion to express his deep need and also to help his devotion.

Our present-day *Oremus* (let us pray) is the survival of a much longer and more detailed exhortation to prayer, such as we still have in the prayers of Good Friday. On Good Friday, we can still see the origin of this usage of *Oremus* when

the priest invites the congregation nine times to pray for temporal needs, such as "let us pray for the king," or "let us pray for heretics," or "for prisoners," or "for peace." The priest or deacon then responds with "Oremus flectamus genua" (let us kneel)— the people then kneel and pray privately for the intention announced until the priest, or sub-deacon, says the word "Levate" (arise)! The priest would then say a prayer aloud, gathering and collecting in one prayer, as it were, the many silent prayers of the congregation. We still have in the Ember-day Masses a reminder of this method. The word "collects" is sometimes given as originating from this "collecting" of the prayer of the people in the celebrant's oration and offering that collection up to God through the public prayer and worship of the Mystical Body's greatest act of worship: the Holy Sacrifice of the Mass.

It ought not be necessary to mention that the people should accept the invitation of the priest to pray with him. The *Oremus* is a call to prayer—a prayer in common which the Savior recommended most earnestly (Matt. 18:20). We are all called to pray the Mass, as Pope St. Pius X exhorts us. Oftentimes, the best method is to pray along with the priest using a prayerbook, preferably Missal. No matter what aids we use, however, we must, at the least, join the priest by praying with him with both our hearts and our minds.

At the end of the *Collect,* the server for the people answers, "Amen," which the Church has transliterated from the original Hebrew, and it means "may it be done so", "assuredly". This *Amen* is not to be neglected by the congregation. Rather, they are urged to say it in their heart and mind. Saying "Amen" expresses their petition and by it they agree to and approve most emphatically what the priest has requested. Providence and the Holy Ghost have seen fit that the Roman rite uses words in Hebrew, Greek, and Latin—the missal is written in Latin, "Kyrie eleison" and "Christe eleison" are kept in their original Greek (as well as parts during Holy Week), while "Amen" (and a few other words, *Alleluia, Hosanna,* and

Sabaoth) are in Hebrew. Thus, whenever we participate in the Holy Mass, all three ancient languages that were written on the Sacred Wood of the Cross, as St. John tells us in John 19:19, are spoken in the words of the Holy Sacrifice of the Mass, and are the media through which we are able to participate in Christ's sacrifice in our present time.

Additionally, other prayers may be added at times to the *Collect* of the day's Mass. This may be done for a few reasons. The most common reason is that the day is also some other feast—whether of Christ, a saint, or several saints—and thus this second feast is commemorated in the day's Mass by being a second Collect of the Mass. Additionally, the Pope or the diocese's bishop may order certain prayers because of some necessity, whether a prayer for good weather, or prayer against persecutors of the Church, a prayer for peace, or something asking for temporal aid. Finally, the priest himself may add an extra collect on non-feast days when a votive Mass is offered.

Questions for Discussion

1. What does this word *Collects* mean?
2. What other names are used in its place?
3. What is meant by a Station? Consult the Catholic Encyclopedia or your Missal for Masses during Lent to find a few of the churches where these Stational Masses occur.
4. Explain the ceremonies performed in the recitation of the *Collects*. Why are ceremonies used?
5. What are the Ember-days? When do they come?
6. Read the long list of prayers in your Missal for Good Friday.
7. What should the congregation do during the *Collects*?
8. Explain the *Amen*.

EPISTLE

We go to Mass not only to pray and to offer sacrifice but also to listen and to learn. We need instruction in our Faith in order to understand and love it more. The *Epistle, Gospel* and Sermon are for the instruction of the people, they are the school in Catholic doctrine. They are made up of readings from the Old and New Testament with an explanation in the sermon.

If one looks at the altar from the pews in the nave, the altar is divided into two halves with respect to a crucifix, which the rubrics require to be facing the priest. Looking from the nave, the *Epistle* is read on the right, or epistle side, of the altar, while the Gospel is read on the left, or Gospel side, of the altar. In the first centuries, insofar as the location allowed, the Christians built their churches so that the altar would be toward the east and priest and people would also be orienting themselves to the east so that everything was looking to the east. In Ezekiel 10, the prophet Ezekiel sees the glory cloud of God depart to the east, and so the Jews looked to the east for the coming of the Messiah. This tradition of facing east has continued for us Christians, in that when we look to the east, we are reminded to prepare for the second coming of Our Lord in the Last Judgment.

The *Epistle* and *Gospel* are read from their respective sides due to the perspective of Christ. From the perspective of Christ on the crucifix, the right—or *Gospel* side of the altar—is to his right, and the Epistle side is to his left. The more honorable side is for the *Gospel, thus the side to the right of the Lord has the Gospel read*. The prominence and superiority of the *Gospel* over the *Epistle* is also emphasized in the fact that the *Epistle* precedes the Gospel, as a foreword precedes so as to introduce a book. The *Epistle,* most often being the words of an apostle or prophet, usually helps to clarify and explain the *Gospel* which is the word of Christ Himself.

After the *Epistle* the server in the name of the congregation answers "Deo gratias," which means "thanks be to God." It is evident that grateful people should give thanks to the Giver of gifts for all His favors, especially for the Scriptures, the Book of Books, the holiest and greatest book this universe can ever produce due to its divine authorship. In Solemn Masses, after his reading of the *Epistle,* the sub-deacon presents the Missal closed to the celebrant, who places his hand on it, and the sub-deacon kisses it. This symbol reflects the fifth chapter of the Book of the Apocalypse and teaches us that Christ, whom the celebrant represents, is the Lamb to whom it is given to unseal the Book which contains His holy mysteries.

Questions for Discussion

1. What is the purpose of the *Epistle* in the Mass?
2. Explain what is meant by an *Epistle?*
3. Consult your New Testament and see who wrote the Epistles. More information on the Epistles can be found in the Catholic Encyclopedia.
4. What should the people do during the *Epistle?*
5. Why does the server answer "Deo Gratias"?

GRADUAL AND ALLELUIA, TRACT, AND SEQUENCE

After the epistle, two short selections are read. For the majority of the liturgical year, the *Gradual* and the *Alleluia* are read. After the *Epistle,* there follows a short selection, usually from a psalm, called the *Gradual.* It is so named for in the early history of the Church, it was sung on the lower step of the reading pulpit, which is called the "gradus" in Latin. The *Gradual* serves as a link between the *Epistle* and the *Gospel*. In the early ages, it is thought that it was introduced to give an opportunity to the congregation to relax and meditate between the long readings from the Bible by highlighting an aspect of the recently read *Epistle* or the day's liturgy for the congregation to focus upon.

Originally only during the Easter season but now extended to all times except in Masses of Lent or Requiems, there *Alleluia*, a cry of great joy, is sung or read. *Alleluia* means, "let us praise the Lord!" and is not a Latin word but a Hebrew word, along with the word *Amen*. These words, along with the *Kyrie*, were not translated into Latin for they are more expressive and vigorous in their original language and some elements of what they mean cannot be concisely translated into another language. The syllable of the *Allelulia* was always very much drawn out, (as are still some modern Amens). This singing of the last "a" of the *Alleluia* in a long series of notes (jubilus) was expressive of great joy. Great joy, like great sorrow, is inarticulate; we often sing and hum without expressing ourselves in words. The singer of the *Alleluia* was expected to know from memory the music for there was no musical notation then. Gradually, words were fitted to the notes of these melodies as an aid to the memory. This system became popular and the words developed into poems or hymns which were sung.

During Eastertide and the Octave of Pentecost, a second Alleluia is added to replace the Gradual so as to show the double portion of joy and praise for the Lord during the most magnificent season of our liturgical year.

The *Tract* is substituted for the *Alleluia* during seasons of mourning and penance. The word *Tract* derives its title from the fact that it was sung in a slow, protracted manner by one singer without any response from the choir so as to show the time of mourning through music by its decreased volume, muted splendor, and increased somberness.

Holy Mother Church, in her wisdom, has decided that some of the greatest days of liturgy—Easter, Pentecost, Corpus Christi, the Seven Sorrows of Our Lady, and the Requiem Mass—should have an additional amount of reflective music and poetry added to them to allow more time and provide more material for the priest and faithful to meditate upon. As the name indicates ("sequential," which means "the following" in Latin, the root of our English words *sequel, sequential,* etc.), the *Sequence* is what follows the *Alleluia* or *Tract*.

At first there were scores of these *Sequences*. When the Propers of the Mass order were simplified under Pope St. Pius V in 1570, only five *Sequences* were kept to help emphasize the most important times in the Church's liturgy. To appreciate these prose-poems, one must read them slowly and thoughtfully. What wealth of doctrine and devotion they contain! They are masterpieces of poetry; simple yet learned; calm yet agitated; dogmatic yet devotional. They are excellent prayers as well, and it would be well for all to use them frequently as prayers. The *Dies Irae* is one of them, and is considered to be the grandest hymn in the Church and is a noble prayer for a good death and merciful judgment; the *Sequence* for Pentecost is a sincere call for the help of the Holy Ghost; the *Stabat Mater* (for some feasts of the Virgin Mary) is a majestic appeal for correct understanding and use of suffering in union with Mary and her Son; the *Lauda Sion* for the feast of Corpus Christi, is a remarkable act of faith in the Eucharist and at the same time an extraordinary prayer that serves as a fitting conclusion to this section:

O Jesus, our Good Shepherd, have mercy on us;
Deign to feed us, to protect us;
Deign to make us see good things
In the land of the living.

Questions for Discussion

1. Explain the *Gradual.*
2. What is meant by the *Alleluia?*
3. What is the *Tract?*
4. Read the five great *Sequences.* (To be found in the Mass for Easter, Pentecost, etc).
5. We suggest study of these *Sequences.* Can you answer why the *Sequence* for Pentecost is considered one of the best and is called the Golden Sequence?
6. Read the article on these Sequences in the Catholic Encyclopedia.
7. What is the history of the *Sequence?*

THE GOSPEL

Before the reading or the singing of the Gospel, the priest at the center of the altar says a beautiful and appropriate prayer to recollect himself and plead for mercy before he reads the Gospel. This is to serve as a preparation for the exalted office of announcing the words of Christ, one of the most noble things we can ever do in this world. The *Gospel* is the good news, the glad tidings, of the Redeemer and His redeeming work. It is the story of Life, of Resurrection, of Heaven: "Behold, I bring you tidings of great joy, that shall be to all the people; for this day is born to you a Savior, who is Christ the Lord" (Luke 11:10).

That he may perform his work in a befitting way, the priest prays three prayers:

> Cleanse my heart and my lips, O Almighty God, who didst cleanse the lips of the Prophet Isaias with a burning coal; vouchsafe so to cleanse me by Thy gracious mercy, that I may be able worthily to proclaim Thy Holy Gospel. Through Christ Our Lord. Amen.
>
> Give me Thy blessing, O Lord!
>
> May the Lord be in my heart and on my lips, that I may worthily and in a becoming manner, announce His Holy Gospel. Amen.

This short string of prayers is drawn from a most impressive event in the life of that generous man of God, Isaias, as recorded in the sixth chapter of his prophecy. One of the Seraphims cleanses the lips of the Prophet with a burning coal from the altar that he might with clean lips join in the song of the angels: "Holy, holy, holy, the Lord God of hosts." It is a good practice for the people to also say this prayer of the priest so that they may humbly and attentively *listen* to the truths of the *Gospel* and profit abundantly therefrom.

Priest Faces North

As you have noticed, while the priest prays the three prayers, the missal is transferred from the Epistle side to the Gospel side, and the missal is put on the corner of the altar at a slight angle. The priest as he reads the *Gospel* is half turned (diagonally) towards the corner of the altar. The Missal itself is turned towards the priest. If the altar was a compass and the priest was facing east when praying the first set of prayers (the Introit, Collect, etc.), why does the priest now face a different direction, towards the north? We have already stated that in the first churches, and in many present day churches, the altar is orientated towards the east, in the direction of the rising sun, which figures Christ, the Light of the World. The priest faces the north at the *Gospel*, for the north represented the land of darkness, of cold, of barren desolation—the land of heathen and those sitting in darkness and in the shadow of death. North is the direction where the Chosen People were taken into captivity, first by the Assyrians and then by the Babylonians. North is the realm of darkness, despair, and exile. The good news of the *Gospel* is the light of truth and warmth of grace to those in the darkness of error and the cold of ignorance, "For it is the power of God unto salvation to every one that believeth, to the Jew first, and to the Greek. For the justice of God is revealed therein" (Romans 1:16).

The south is the region of warmth, of life, the land of growth and harvest and joy, the land of grace and blessing through Christ's life. "The Lord shall send out His word, and shall melt them; His winds shall blow,—and the waters shall run" (Psalms 147:18).

At the *Gospel* the priest prayerfully greets the people with the sincere wish, "The Lord be with you." May truth come to you and dwell within you and bring forth wholesome and plentiful fruit in His name! Then is made over the first words of the sacred reading the Sign of the Cross with the thumb. This signifies that the cross is the completion of the *Gospel*; it is its strength and its virtue. The cross preaches the *Gospel*; it represents the words and works of the Master; the cross is the Gospel.

The Triple Blessing

This Sign of the Cross the priest repeats on his forehead, on his lips, and on his breast. This beautiful ceremony is eloquent

and is ripe with signification. The signing of the forehead means we must know the teachings of Christ and His Church and we must firmly believe in His Word. The signing of the lips means that we are to speak the Savior's teaching, to defend Him everywhere, to announce His saving words to others, to live His life. The signing of the breast means that we are to love Him with all our heart. Oh, that we may have a living faith in Jesus! Jesus "Who humbled himself becoming obedient unto death, even to the death of the cross. For which cause God also hath exalted him and hath given him a name which is above all names: that in the name of Jesus every knee should bow . . . and every tongue should confess that the Lord Jesus Christ is the glory of God the Father" (Philippians 2:8). In short, this triple signing shows that we love the Lord with all of our heart, soul, strength, and mind.

At the reading of the Gospel, all stand to express their reverence and respect for the Word of God, "the sword of the Spirit" (Ephesians 6:17). This recalls the reading of the Law after it had been lost for many years: "Then Esdras the priest brought the law before the multitude of men and women, and all those that could understand, in the first day of the seventh month. And he read it plainly in the street that was before the water gate, from the morning until midday, before the men, and the women, and all those that could understand: and the ears of all the people were attentive to the book. And Esdras the scribe stood upon a step of wood, which he had made to speak upon. . . And Esdras opened the book before all the people: for he was above all the people: and when he had opened it, all the people stood" (2 Ezra 8:2–5). We stand to show also our eager attention and heartfelt interest in His message.

At the conclusion, the congregation responds through the words of the server, "Praise be to Thee, O Christ!" We praise and thank the Savior for having announced the good tidings to us ignorant and poor. "To heal the contrite of heart; to preach deliverance to the captives; to set at liberty them that are bruised: to preach the acceptable year of the Lord, and the day of reward" (Luke 4:19).

The priest on finishing the reading, kisses the first words of the sacred text and says, "By virtue of the words of the Gospel may our sins be blotted out," which is omitted at Requiems as all prayers are directed and are meant to profit the deceased.

In order to realize what great devotion we should have for the Bible and its reading, let us see the mind of the Church as expressed so vividly in the singing of the *Gospel* at a Solemn Mass in the words of Father Keenan:

> The deacon of the Mass is about to sing the Gospel. Reverently he places the book on the altar beside the Tabernacle, and, profoundly inclined, kneels before the two to pray that his heart and lips may be purified, as the communicant of the day has purified heart and lips by penance and fasting. Solemnly raising the book to his heart, he kneels before the celebrant to receive the blessing, and proceeds in solemn procession to the place of honor, the right of the Tabernacle. No reading-table is used; a consecrated sub-deacon holds the opened book in his arms, resting it on his forehead that he may obliterate himself and serve impersonally, while acolytes stand on either side with lighted candles to remind all that the Light of the World is to be shed anew in brightness and beauty. The deacon solemnly invokes the Spirit of God upon all the hearers; still he pauses; he makes the Sign of the Cross on the page opened before him, on his own forehead, lips and heart that the sign of Christ may seal the solemn reading. Taking the censor with incense blessed in the Name of Him in Whose honor it is offered, he

incenses the book three times, the liturgical offering to Christ. In the religious chant of the Church he solemnly sings the Inspired Word appointed for the day; at each mention of the Holy Name of Jesus, the celebrant, standing at the altar, reverently bows to the cross, symbol of the same Christ contained in the book. At the end the sub-deacon, his impersonal function completed, reverently carries the book back to the altar, and hands it to the celebrant, who kisses it with loving devotion in the name of the entire congregation, standing at reverent attention.

"What does it all mean? It is the Catholic Church's expression of her deep reverence for the Bible. She is saying to her children: The Word of God is Christ."[1]

Questions for Discussion

1. What is meant by a Gospel? Who wrote them? When and why? Where are they to be found?
2. Explain the *Munda Cor Meum.*
3. Read Isaiah, chapter 6.
4. Why does the priest face northward (or somewhat turned) at the reading of the Gospel?
5. Explain the Sign of the Cross with the thumb at the *Gospel?*
6. What should the attitude of the congregation be during the *Gospel?*
7. Why does the celebrant kiss the Missal at the end?
8. Explain the elaborate ceremonies at the singing of the *Gospel* at a Solemn Mass.
9. Why should we read the Bible daily at home?

---

1 Rev. Dr. Francis L. Keenan, *The Story of the Bible,* page 16.

THE CREDO

We have finished our explanation of the first part of the Mass. The Mass is divided into two parts, the Mass of the Catechumens and the Mass of the Faithful. The first section is the Mass of the Catechumens, for it originally was chiefly for the instruction of those not yet baptized (the catechumens) and was structured around studying catechism. This first part of the Mass is modeled mainly according to the Synagogue service of the Jews in exile, as this service for the Jews outside Jerusalem was made up of prayer, of the chanting of Psalms and of readings from the Bible since they could not worship within the Temple. The Church adopted this, but Christianized it, and enlarged its scope. Over the passage of time, its spirit deepened and new Christian prayers and hymns were added with readings from the New Testament.

After the sermon, the catechumens (the non-baptized) were dismissed and only the baptized faithful were allowed to remain for the rest of the service, the offering of Sacrifice. The non-baptized were told to leave since they could not take part in the Sacrifice for they were not yet fully instructed in its meaning and grandeur and they likewise could not partake of the Communion which was the usual practice of the faithful at every Mass in the early Church. Nowadays, the dismissal of non-baptized persons after the sermon is no longer the practice, but they are to still to refrain from receiving Holy Communion.

The Mass of the Catechumens serves as an excellent introduction to the Sacrifice. Through it the faithful are elevated in mind and heart to its high level. It is a preparation-prayer. It is like the preface to a book, a prelude to a play, an overture to an opera. We have already analyzed the various parts of this section of the Mass, may we again urge all who attend, to religiously enter into the spirit and purpose of this introductory section. A good preparation leads to a good ending.

Very appropriately, after the readings from the Bible and the hearing of the sermon, the *Credo* (Latin for "I believe") or profession of faith comes. A Creed embodies the principle tenets of a religion, and is a meet and just way to show our orthodoxy in submitting to the Church and her teachings before entering into the offering of sacrifice. The Creed that we sing is the Nicene Creed, first composed and promulgated at the Council of Nicaea and then later adapted in its present form at the First Council of Constantinople in 381. The people have heard the truths of their religion— now they affirm their belief in them. Frequent saying of the Apostles' Creed or the Nicene Creed is a strong stimulus to faith, especially when recited by groups. The *Credo* appears at a very fitting time in the Mass—at the beginning of the Sacrifice. The Mass is the Mystery of Faith, the Sacrifice of Calvary represented, a memorial of the Redeemer's passion and death. The *Credo* is an act of faith in the principal truths of our religion which pass in review during the Mass.

Questions for Discussion

1. What are the two main divisions of the Mass?
2. What is meant by the Mass of the Catechumens?
3. What is the purpose of the first section of the Mass, that is, from the Psalm 42 to the Offertory?
4. What should be the thoughts and prayers of the people in attendance during this part?
5. Why is the *Credo* said in some Masses?

Offertory

Offertory Prayers

The Meaning of Sacrifice

The Mass, we have heard so frequently, is a sacrifice. Now a sacrifice, in a few words, is the giving of a gift through a priest, to God. We give these gifts in order to express, to show publicly, our intention and mind: to adore and praise God, to thank Him, to ask Him to supply our needs, and to make reparation for sins. In short, adoration, thanksgiving, petition, and reparation. In the very first of these pages on the Mass, we wrote why people make visible expressions of their inward feelings and this is most nobly expressed through the act of sacrifice. In a sacrifice, we give to God something that can be handled, seen, felt, and tasted. This gift stands for our interior sentiments and wishes of praise, thanks, and sorrow before God. Just as good children give gifts to their parents and as friends give gifts, so do the children and friends of God give Him gifts; for a gift expresses more powerfully and eloquently than mere halting, stumbling words the mind of the giver. It is easy to talk; it is easy to deceive in speech. Words cost nothing. Giving gifts means work—they mean sacrifice. Gifts are hard to give, as a rule; therefore, their greater worth.

At the Mass, we give the gifts of bread and of wine. These gifts of ours, in a few moments, become the Body and Blood of Christ, the Son of God. So we give to God the Father His Son, under the appearances of bread and of wine, the best Gift possible. Just why do we offer wine and bread? Because bread and wine are the staff of life. They are the staple items of food. People the world over eat bread. Nearly all people, in the time of Christ—and still in most lands—take wine as a usual drink. Bread and wine represent, symbolize, most aptly our life which we owe to God and by whom it is to be some day judged.

Bread and wine also express the unity, the oneness of the Church. Just as bread is made from many grains of wheat, just as wine is made from many grapes, so is the Church made up of many members. All Catholics are to be one in faith, in obedience and, most especially, in charity. All Christians are to love one another, to be of one mind and heart, as Christ loved us.

In the first centuries of the Church, the people at Mass brought their gifts of bread and wine to the altar rail. There at the Offertory, the priests with the bishop would collect the bread in large cloths like table cloths, and the wine was poured into large, two-handled chalices. These were brought to the altar. Sufficient bread and wine for the Mass and Communion of the people was kept at the altar. The remainder afterwards, was given to the poor.

Everyone in the church—priests and people—would make an offering to declare and show their participation in the common sacrifice of the Mass. They gave their gifts to express their praise, their thanks, their prayer, their sorrow to God. Their dedication to God was more meaningful and more satisfying when made by way of a gift than by words. The gifts are given publicly for the public society belongs to God and must worship as well as the individual.

Today, the procession of the people bringing their gifts to the sanctuary no longer occurs. However, in some European parishes and in some American convents and monasteries, it is being held. Such a beautiful ceremony should be revived. A memory of this old custom still is found in the ordination of priests when they present a candle to the bishop; and in the consecration of a bishop, when he gives to the consecrating bishop two loaves of bread, two small casks of wine and two candles. Now at the Offertory, on Sundays and Feast-days, the collection is taken. People now give an offering in money, for it is much more handy for everyone to give money than to give wine, or bread, or candles, etc. People will give more and give more eagerly when they realize that their gift of money may be taken as their gift to God in the Mass. It is the expression of their sorrow, their thanks, their praise to God. What we can give, we give. We give the most we can; not the least we can. Who, after all, has done the greatest good to us? Is it not the Lord God, who suffered and died for us? Then to God, in appreciation, give the best we have.

When people give their offerings with such feelings and sentiments, naturally, their participation in the Mass is more intimate and their share, richer. Likewise, they take greater interest in the Mass. A sacrifice is a gift to God—there is no sacrifice without a gift. At least on Sundays and on feast days, we intend to make a generous gift to show outwardly our inward sacrifice.

We have seen the idea of the *Offertory*, that is, the spirit of the offering in a sacrifice. At the beginning of the *Offertory* of the Mass, the priest says, "Dominus vobiscum"—the Lord be with you. The phrase *Dominus vobiscum* reminds us of our English greeting "good-bye," the shortened form of "God be with you." At every important turn in the Mass, the priest in prayer wishes the Lord to be with the congregation, to help them take part as correctly and as faithfully as possible. The people, of course, should in politeness answer their celebrant in the prayer, "And with thy spirit", that is, "May the Lord be with you also, Father." Now at the *Offertory*, the priest prays that the people be attentive to their Mass, that they dedicate themselves to God; that they enter into the spirit of sacrifice.

Offering of the Bread

After the "Oremus"—let us pray—the priest says the offertory antiphon. What remains at the present time of this antiphon is a much shortened form of a longer chant which was sung in the early Church. We mentioned already the beautiful old custom of the people bringing their offerings for the Mass and their Communion to the sanctuary. During this procession, which took some moments, the choir chanted some suitable text, usually from the Psalms. This offertory antiphon or verse changes with the variable parts of the Mass at different seasons of the Church year, and at Masses for saints and feasts. Its purpose is to give the idea or prevailing note of that particular Mass, in other words, to give the main thought in the feast commemorated or in the saint honored. It sort of returns to our memories the *Introit* lest we forget the day's saint or feast, and highlights a thought for us to focus upon during the offering of the bread and wine.

Requiem Offertory Long

The *Offertory* verse at Requiem Masses is the only one which has kept its original text. It gives an idea of the prayer element of these antiphons. In it, we pray for the dead. The language, we must remember, is very realistic and vivid and the deceased are presented as still in life, lying on their death bed and dying. We pray that the person be saved "from the lion's mouth, lest hell swallow them, etc." We do not pray that the souls in hell be saved, for they cannot, but we pray, in the bright language of the liturgy, that the souls in Purgatory be granted peace, and the living, a happy death. The *Requiem Offertory* chant is not only for the peaceful rest of the suffering souls, but for the instruction of the living as well so that they too can reach their heavenly home.

Offertory Prayers

The three principal parts of the Mass are the Offertory, Consecration, and Communion. At the *Offertory*, the gifts or the offerings are prepared for the sacrifice, for the Consecration. The offerings are sanctified, are blessed that they may be fit and decent gifts. They are withdrawn from their ordinary use and set aside for a more noble purpose—to be changed soon into the Body and Blood of Christ. The Church blesses and sanctifies everything that she uses. Christ at the Last Supper, taking the bread and wine and raising His eyes to Heaven, blessed them. The priest at the Offertory blesses the offerings and dedicates them to God.

The celebrant now takes the paten (the gold-plated disc or saucer-like plate) with the host upon it, raises his eyes to the crucifix, lowers his eyes, and then says the prayer:

> Accept, O holy Father, Almighty and eternal God, this unspotted Host, which I, Thy unworthy servant offer unto Thee, my living and true God, for my innumerable sins, offenses and negligences and for all here present; as also for all faithful Christians, both living and dead, that it may avail both me and them for salvation unto life everlasting. Amen.

The Mass is offered to God, the Almighty and eternal, the living and true God. We believe in one God who really exists. Ours is not the belief of pagans who believe in several gods; or who make gods of things in creation as the sun, trees, rocks, animals, etc. This prayer is offered to the Father first as it is fitting to address Him first since He is the First Person in the Trinity. Subsequent prayers will later be addressed to the Second Person, God the Son in the prayer during the blessing of the water, and to the Third Person, God the Holy Spirit, in the "Veni, Sanctificator." Finally, the entire Trinity will be invoked in the last prayer of the Offertory before the *Orate Fratres*.

The host is called spotless, not only because it is set aside for this Sacrifice, but also—and especially—because the Church already regards it as the Body of Christ. The Church looks ahead a few moments and anticipates the Consecration when this bread is to be truly spotless, immaculate, pure—His Body. We already see upon the paten the sinless and stainless Savior. The gifts are called spotless not by reason of what they are now, but of what they are soon to become.

In this offertory prayer, the priest prays for himself, "for my innumerable sins, offences and negligences." He is the priest; he is the minister of Christ, His spokesman; he is the official representative of the people. Therefore, he must pray for himself, for "he himself also is compassed with infirmity" (Hebrews 5:2). The priest realizes that only he who is "innocent in hands, and clean of heart" may "go up to the mountain of the Lord, and stand in His holy place" (Psalm 23).

The priest offers the Mass also "for all here present". Those nearest to a big fire get most warmth out of it; likewise, the people present at Mass derive, next to the priest, the most fruit, provided they are interested in following the Mass and praying it with the celebrant.

The kind Mother, the Church, prays for all, "also for all faithful Christians, both living and dead". Everyone benefits from the Mass in proportion to his devotion and closeness to It. It should be needless to say that while at Mass—and we must try to attend daily—we ought to take active part in sincerely offering the gifts of bread and wine, and that we are not to offer them alone. Indeed, we are called to offer more: ourselves and Christ to the Father.

See how kind and charitable is the Church! We must be like Her—filled with charity. We are, remember, members of the Mystical Body of Christ; we are brothers of Christ and therefore, brothers to one another. In all our prayers, henceforth, we will pray for "all faithful Christians, both living and dead."

In a similar manner, we are strongly urged to make each morning what we call the Morning Offering. In it, we offer to God all the Masses said throughout the world that day. The Mass is for all the people, and we share more abundantly in all the Masses when we take more active part in them. In some parishes, the tower bell is tolled at the Consecration. This reminds people at home to pause what they are doing, unite themselves with the intentions of the Mass, and to offer the Mass with all of its offerings and fruits to God.

Questions for Discussion

1. Just what do you mean by a sacrifice? By the Mass as a sacrifice? Why do we offer sacrifice?
2. Explain why bread and wine have been chosen to be presented at this time.

3. What is the fundamental reason for the offertory collection?
4. What should be the thought of the people during the first part of the *Offertory?* What is the reason and purpose of an *Offertory?*
5. What is the *Offertory* antiphon? Explain the one said in a Requiem.
6. For whom is the Mass offered? Explain in detail the prayers said at the offering of the bread.
7. Do we share in every Mass said? Do the departed in Purgatory? How do we take part in every Mass?

Offering of the Wine

Now the priest goes to the epistle side where he receives from the altar-boy water and wine. A few drops of water are poured into the wine, while the celebrant recites:

> O God, who in creating human nature, hast wonderfully dignified it, and still more wonderfully reformed it! grant that by the mystery of this water and wine, we may be made partakers of the divine nature of Him, who vouchsafed to become partaker of our human nature, namely, Jesus Christ, Our Lord Thy Son, who liveth and reigneth with Thee, etc. Amen.

Why is a little water poured into the wine? It is said from Apostolic Tradition that Christ, following the Jewish custom, mixed a little water with the wine at the Last Supper. In fact, it has been determined to be such a sacred part of the rite, that if the priest purposefully neglects to put water in the wine, the Council of Trent says it would be a grave sin on the priest's part. The Church follows then the example of Christ. The water and the wine also recall to mind the water and blood which flowed from the Savior's side on being opened by the soldier's lance.

The water represents the people; the wine is for Christ. The mixing of the wine with a little water brings out the teaching regarding our unity, our oneness, with Christ. As the water is lost in the wine, so do good Christians become lost in, or one with, Christ. The water becomes wine; we by grace, become other Christs by being incorporated to Christ.

The meaning of this ceremony is explained in the accompanying prayer: "Grant that by the mystery of this water and wine (as the little water becomes wine), we may be made partakers of the divine nature of Him." One of the best fruits from the Mass is an increase in sanctifying grace. St. Peter says by grace we are "made partakers of the divine nature" (2 Peter 1:4). Through grace we become sharers in His divine life. We are made gods; we are deified, divinized (John 10:34, 35). By grace we become the adopted children of God and the brothers of Christ (Romans 8:15 sq; Galatians 4:4 sq).

This ceremony of the commingling of the water and wine is one of the most eloquent in the Mass. It tells us so much and so divinely. It tells all about grace—and that is always divine. It tells of the mystical Body of Christ which is the Church. How we should love one another! "See how these Christians love one another." It tells of the creation of man in innocence, in grace, in freedom from human troubles, sorrows and evils. It tells about the Incarnation, "Who became partaker of our human nature". God became man that men might become gods. It speaks of the Redemption, "and still more wonderfully reformed" (our human nature).

So during this extraordinary ceremony, we think of our dignity—brothers of Christ through grace. We think of the destruction of sin. We thank Christ for His life and sufferings. We beg for an increase in grace, and help to become more and more Christ-like.

Blessing of the Water

Before the priest accepts from the altar-boy the water, he makes over it the Sign of the Cross. Why? The water stands for the people, and they, due to their weak human nature, do need blessings and sanctification before their union with Christ who is represented by the wine, and thus the wine is not blessed. Additionally, the blessing of the water calls to mind the human nature that was blessed when Christ assumed it in the Incarnation, uniting the two natures in the one Divine Person in a similar way to how water and wine are united when in the chalice of the priest. In a Requiem Mass, the blessing of the water is omitted for in these Masses all references to the living, as far as possible, are omitted, and all blessings are given to or for the dead. All attention is called to the dead insofar as it is possible.

Offering of the Chalice

The priest raises the chalice in presentation to God and says the offering prayer:

> We offer unto Thee, O Lord, the Chalice of salvation, beseeching Thy clemency, that it may ascend before Thy divine Majesty, as a sweet odor for our salvation, and for that of the whole world. Amen.

"We offer." There are two who offer this sacrifice—the priest and the people. Christ, of course, is the High-priest, and the priest and people offer with Christ this Sacrifice. Too many of the laity in the congregation let the priest do everything; they simply sit in their places and "hear" Mass without praying the Mass. There is more to Mass than simply "hearing" it. It is a sacrifice of priest and people and consequently, the people are to realize they are priests as it were, and are to join with the priest in saying the prayers and in making the offering of the Mass their own prayer.

"But you are a chosen generation, a kingly priesthood, a holy nation, a purchased people" (1 Peter 2:9). We are priests, not ordained as priests are, but we are priests since we are baptized and confirmed and have received Christ in grace. We are servants, creatures of God, and must offer to Him sacrifice. At Mass, we, in our way, join with the official spokesman, the priest, in presenting to God, the Creator, our gifts that we have received from His bounty and that we freely give back to Him.

In the offering of the chalice, we pray, as in the offering of the host, for the "whole world." We are Catholics, members of the universal Church; we are brothers of Christ, brothers to one another, and we pray for one another since the interest of one is the interest of all. We offer the "Chalice of salvation." We anticipate the Consecration. We already regard the chalice as containing the saving blood of the Redeemer. It is the "Chalice of salvation" by reason of the intimate and immediate relation between wine that is there now and the Precious Blood that is presently to take its place.

In a Solemn High Mass, you may have noticed the deacon assisting the celebrant in raising the chalice at the Offertory. This ceremony brings out and stresses the "we" in the prayer and in the offering. The deacon represents the people. The people, through the deacon, and the celebrant both offer the sacrifice of the Mass. The Mass is not an action of the priest alone—it is for the people also. They must unite themselves with the priest and Christ in offering the Mass.

After the offering of the chalice, there follows another marvelous prayer:

"In a spirit of humility and with a contrite heart, may we be accepted by Thee, O Lord, and may our Sacrifice be so offered in Thy sight this day as to please Thee."

The gifts we give to God are symbolical, representative of ourselves, our souls, our life. Gifts express exteriorly what we feel and are interiorly, spiritually. They only express interior sacrifice. So if we are not humble and contrite at heart, our sacrifice is a lie and it means little. "If therefore thou offer thy gift at the altar, and there thou remember that thy brother hath anything against thee; leave there thy offering before the altar, and go first to be reconciled to thy brother, and then coming thou shalt offer thy gift" (Matt. 5:23, 24).

We ask God to accept us according to our humility and contrition. Naturally, if we are in sin, if we are not repentant, if we have love for even little faults, we do not carry away much from the Mass. We cheat ourselves. If we do not empty ourselves of evil, we cannot be filled with the living waters of grace. If we have not decreased sin in ourselves, we cannot have grace increase in ourselves. Now we understand, probably, a bit better why all those preparatory prayers in the first part of the Mass. We see now the purpose of the *Confiteor*, the *Kyrie*, the *Credo*. "A sacrifice to God is an afflicted spirit: a contrite and humble heart thou wilt not despise, O Lord" (Psalm 50). We ask in the prayer that our "Sacrifice be so offered in Thy sight as to please Thee." How can it be pleasing to God and profitable to us, when we come to church with feelings of hatred, lack of charity, disobedience and all sorts of ill-will? It is like the sacrifice of Cain with which God was not pleased, for he offered to God what was cheap, and did not offer his best, did not offer freely, did not offer the finest representation of himself.

In this sublime prayer, we ask, "may we be accepted by Thee, O Lord." What is after all the gift we bring to the altar? After all, we place OURSELVES on the paten and in the chalice. WE are the victims; WE are the bread and the wine. "I beseech you brethren that you present your bodies a living sacrifice, holy, pleasing unto God, your reasonable service" (Romans 12:1). We give ourselves to God. That is what He wants. We give our life, our senses, our body, our memory, our will, our intellect; we give all we have to Him. We dedicate our service; our vocation to Him. At the Consecration, we become one with Christ and pleasing to the Father.

You have noticed, no doubt, in these offertory prayers, the repeated expressions of giving, of offering, of acceptance by God. How often we go to Mass with the idea of getting and receiving uppermost in our intention. Mass is a sacrifice and a sacrifice is a giving, a destruction. It is giving to God of our worship, our adoration, thanks, petition, and reparation. It is giving to God, of ourselves, our life. And when we have given ourself, then only are we ready and somewhat worthy, to receive from God grace and help. We are forever asking and begging—and it is proper—but how rarely do we give adoration, service and thanks! Why ask so much and so often from God when we give so little and so rarely?

Questions for Discussion

1. Why is a little water poured into the wine?
2. Explain in detail the prayer said during the ceremony.

3. What is sanctifying grace? What does it do for one? Is it worthwhile? How can we grow in grace? (Read advanced catechisms and the article in the Catholic Encyclopedia).
4. Read 2 Peter 1:4; John 10:34, 35; Romans 8:15 sq.; Galatians 4:4; 1 John 3:1.
5. What is meant by the expression "Mystical Body of Christ"?
6. Why is the water not blessed in a Requiem?
7. Explain the prayer said at the offering of the wine?
8. Who offers the sacrifice of the Mass? Explain.
9. Are the people priests? Explain.
10. Explain in detail "in a spirit of humility and contrition of heart".
11. Explain Matthew 5:23 sq. Do we benefit much from the Mass when we are uncharitable? Why not?
12. Explain Romans 12:1. How does it relate to the Mass?
13. Read the *Following of Christ*: Book IV, Ch. 8–9.
14. What is meant by the "we" prayers? Why should the people use a Missal at Mass?
15. What should be the mind and prayer of the people during the Offertory?

The Lavabo

After handling the gifts and the vessels (remember, formerly the celebrant received the offertory gifts from everyone present at Mass), and after the incensing at Solemn Mass, it is but natural that the celebrant should wash his hands. Not only might his fingers be a bit dirty from the handling of the thurible, but also he is rapidly approaching the culmination of Mass and the *raison d'etre* for his priesthood: the Consecration is soon to occur. The priest realizes the importance of purity, both inwardly and outwardly, in his relations to the Body of Christ. He must be clean, especially of soul, to the greatest degree possible. This sincere desire is expressed in the washing of the tips of his fingers and in the prayer:

> I will wash my hands in innocence:
> That I may hear the voice of praise,
> O Lord, I have loved the beauty of Thy house, and the place where Thy glory dwelleth.

This is part of Psalm 25, and the priest recited the entire second half of it before proceeding in the Mass. David wrote it to express his intense desire to be worthy to appear in the temple and to offer sacrifice. The priest washes his fingers to symbolize the spiritual cleanness he strives to live each day, and to ask God for the graces needed to purify his soul even further so that he can worthily offer the oblation. He wishes to wash his soul of all uncleanness, even to the very tips of his fingers. Christ at the Last Supper washed the feet of His apostles to tell them in striking and memorable manner the need of purity of soul. "Who shall ascend into the mountain of the Lord: or who shall stand in His holy place? The innocent of hands and clean of heart" (Psalm 23). Pilate washed his hands after condemning Christ to express his innocence in His trial. But Pilate was not innocent. The washing was a lie. Let our washing of the fingers be more honest! "Wash me yet more from my iniquity, and cleanse me from sin" (Psalm 50), let us call to mind the purity we need to worthily participate in the holiest actions the universe can produce: the bringing down of the God-man into our very presence.

Receive, O Holy Trinity

The priest returns to the center of the altar, bows, and addresses a prayer to the Holy Trinity. He begs the Trinity to receive these gifts, this sacrifice offered in memory of the Passion, Resurrection, and Ascension of Our Lord. The Mass, you know, is also a memorial of the Passion, the Pascal Mystery. But it also recalls to us His redemptive death on Calvary which opened for us the gates of Heaven, but it also recalls to us the fruit of His Passion—His Resurrection and Ascension—the two miracles by which the Father declares His love for the Son and the acceptance of, and pleasure in, His atoning life by which alone mankind is saved. We also at Mass wish to thank God for the gift of the Redemption.

We offer the Mass also in honor of the saints. The priest here lists a great number of saints: Our Lady, St. John the Baptist, Saints Peter and Paul, the saints in the altar stone upon which Mass is offered, and all of the communion of saints. The saints are Christ's friends, are united to Him, are the greatest reflections of Him, are with Him. When Christ is honored, they are honored with Him since they are members of His mystical body, and have participated in it more fully than most men on earth have, and are a witness to that. We cannot by the Mass and our prayers increase their glory in Heaven, but by our invocation of the saints we can increase their honor upon earth. This is called their accidental glory. We can make them better known and loved by the people on earth, and help people to better love God by their example of loving God that they gave while here in this valley of tears: in that way we honor them.

In this final prayer of the offertory, we beg the saints to intercede for us. They are the friends of the Savior; they are close to the King; therefore, they have influence with Him. The Lord answers their prayers in appreciation for their heroic lives and years of loyal service. We can go to Christ directly with our requests, it is true, but He wishes us to invoke His saints. In this way we are brought to imitate their holy example. In this way, they are honored by us and by Him.

Questions for Discussion

1. Why does the celebrant wash his fingers?
2. Explain Psalm 25's purpose in the Mass.
3. What is meant in saying, "the Mass is a memorial of the Passion"?
4. How does the Mass honor the saints?
5. What is meant by the Communion of the Saints? Why should we honor the saints? What is the best way of honoring them outside the Mass?

THE ORATE FRATRES

The priesthood of all the faithful is expressed in the *Orate Fratres*. The priest, turning to the congregation, reminds them that the Mass is *their* sacrifice as well as his. He asks them—rather, commands them to join him in prayer. It is not an exhortation, but a directive: Pray! The prayers of offering and presentation have been recited and the time for the Consecration is approaching. The celebrant realizes this. He needs help. He turns and addresses the faithful:

Pray brethren, that my sacrifice and yours may be acceptable to God, the Father Almighty.

The priest calls them "brethren", and so they are. Did not Christ teach the Apostles to pray, "Our Father, who art in Heaven"? "Behold what manner of charity the Father hath bestowed upon us, that we should be called, and should be the sons of God" (1 John 3:1). Certainly the priest needs help. He is human: he falls. "He himself (the priest) also is compassed with infirmity" (Hebrews 5:2). Shall not his brothers pray for him?

Yes, the faithful will pray for their priest, and they, through the server, answer:

> May the Lord receive the Sacrifice from thy hands, to the praise and glory of His name, to our benefit and to that of all His Holy Church.

This is the prayer of each person in attendance: the faithful gathered, the angels present, the saints surrounding the altar of God. To this generous and heartfelt prayer, the celebrant answers gratefully, "Amen." May it be done so. We all know the Mass as the Sacrifice of the Savior is most pleasing and acceptable to the Father. But from the human side, from the contribution of the visible ministers and people, the Mass, perfect in itself, can become imperfect. Little wonder priest and people pray for each other that they may be well enriched in this Mass and also give much glory and honor to God and no dishonor. "But I am needy and poor; O God make haste to help me!"

"My Sacrifice and yours". The Mass is for both priest and people. "Because he himself also is compassed with infirmity . . . And therefore he ought, as for the people, so also for himself, to offer for sins" (Hebrews 5:3).

You have noticed that this prayer, *Pray, brethren,* is a "we" prayer. It states that the Sacrifice is *our* Sacrifice—"my Sacrifice and yours". The Mass is not a spectacle to watch, or a theatrical performance to admire—it is our Sacrifice, it is our giving of ourselves it is our "reasonable service" (Romans 12:1). We have several times called attention to the need of realizing that the Mass is a Sacrifice and consequently it must be offered by the people with and through the priest, through Christ. The faithful co-offer with the priest. They must present the Sacrifice to the Father. "You are a royal priesthood", says St. Peter (1 Peter, 2:9). You are priests (not ordained in Holy Orders) since you are one with Christ in Baptism and Confirmation and you have received the priesthood of Christ.

There is a book by Karl Adam, *The Spirit of Catholicism,* which everyone should read. On page 126 in the 1929 edition, he writes, "Every baptism is a consecration to the priesthood of Christ, for baptism removes the man from the profane world, appropriates him to Christ and sanctifies him for the performance of those most general acts of worship which belong to the vocation of the child of God. And the sacramental character of Confirmation intensifies this priesthood, since it fits the Christian to take an active share in the building of the temple of God." These two sacraments do not merely confer grace, but also impart to the soul an abiding religious character whereby the soul is incorporated in the priesthood of Christ. You remember these teachings from your instructions on the sacramental character—that indelible mark impressed in these two sacraments is a participation in the priesthood of Christ. Through these marks imprinted upon our souls for all eternity, we can truly call this sacrifice our own and we can truly offer it up in the ways that these characters, these sacramental imprints, allow, nay, command!

We Must Offer Mass

Now you understand a little better why you are constantly being told to be attentive at Mass, to be interested, to take part in the Mass. Attending Mass is active, not passive. You are priests; you must present your gifts with the priest to God. We must not simply "hear" Mass, we must offer it! We must participate actively, offering in union with our Lord the homage and devotion and service of our daily life. These gifts we bring to the altar, represented outwardly by bread and wine, so that as the bread and wine are changed into the Body and Blood of Christ we ourselves may be consumed as victims in His great Sacrifice; this is what St. Paul tells us in that first verse of the twelfth chapter of his Epistle to the Romans that sums up all of Christianity: "I beseech you therefore, brethren, by the mercy of God, that you present your bodies a living sacrifice, holy, pleasing unto God, your reasonable service."

That is the content and meaning of the Mass prayers. In order that you enter into the spirit of sacrifice and the Mass, we entreat you to follow the Mass with a Mass prayerbook, the Missal. Do not pray AT Mass but pray THE Mass.

Questions for Discussion

1. Explain the invitation made to the people. Explain the response of the people.
2. Explain how this prayer is a "we" prayer.
3. What is meant by the priesthood of the people? What follows from that?
4. Do the people offer the Mass? Why?

5. Should the people pray the Mass? Why?
6. Explain the selection from *The Spirit of Catholicism*.

THE SECRET

Now the priest prays silently. No more will he turn toward the people until after the Communion, for his focus is on offering these gifts to the Most High. The *Secret* prayers are said in a faint and quiet voice. They are prayers which invoke God's blessing on the gifts and on ourselves, that through them we may gain rich fruit. They are called the *Secret* because they are said over the gifts set apart—the *oblata secreta*.

Let us give two fine examples of a *Secret* prayer. Notice how we pray that the gifts may be acceptable and pleasing; and also express the giver's sentiments:

Regard, O Lord, the unutterable love of the Heart of Thy beloved Son, so that what we offer may be an acceptable gift to Thee, and an atonement for our sins. (Feast of the Sacred Heart).

This one for Passion Sunday is remarkable:

> May these gifts, O Lord, unloose the bonds of our wickedness, and win for us the gifts of Thy mercy.

For further examples, see the Sundays before Lent, and Corpus Christi. Each Secret is worthy of meditation and is there to help us more worthily enter into the Canon of the Mass, the Holy of Holies, the portal for us to do what Moses could not: come face to face with God Almighty.

Questions for Discussion

1. Explain what is meant by the *Secret* prayer.

2. What is its spirit? Why said in secret?
3. Read and explain the *Secrets* for the Sundays in Advent, Epiphany season and Lent.

The Consecration

The Preface and Sanctus

The Offertory is finished and we are about to begin the *Consecration*. We saw in the *Offertory* a preparation, a getting-ready of the gifts. We brought our gifts of bread and wine to the altar and begged God to accept them as expressions, as symbols of a humble and contrite heart, in accord with St. Paul entreats us to do daily: "I beseech you brethren, that you present your bodies a living sacrifice, holy, pleasing unto God, your reasonable service" (Romans 12:1). We cannot recall too often that the gifts of bread and wine, the outward sacrifice, stand for the inward sacrifice, our sentiments of sorrow, thanks, adoration, etc. The inward sacrifice is the reality which counts; the outward is but a sign. To have a true and complete sacrifice the two must be wedded.

Prayer Is Introduction

In the Consecration, our gifts become the Body and Blood of Christ; our gift, or sacrifice, is pleasing because it is Christ. To help us enter into the spirit of sacrifice; to help our attention, the Church gives us the *Preface*. As the word indicates, this prayer is an introduction to what follows. Similar to the introduction of a speech, to the preface of a book, it tells about and prepares for what follows. It disposes us for a profitable reading or appreciation of the contents to come in accordance with the day's liturgy.

Opens with Dialogue

The *Preface* opens with an intimate and tender dialogue between the faithful and their priest, "The Lord be with you". "And with thy spirit". Notice what happens first: they pray for each other. They both need help now to sacrifice well. Both—especially the priest—are on holy ground and are very soon to be in His presence. The priest no more turns towards the people to greet them. He is occupied with the altar exclusively. He has now, like Moses on Mount Sinai, entered the holy cloud. He sees only God.

At the words, "Lift up your hearts", the priest raises his hands to express his yearning after what is heavenly and the good which only heaven can give. "Let us lift up our hearts with our hands to the Lord in the heavens" (Lamentations 3:41). The people answer, "We do lift them up to God". May their response be sincere and well intentioned! In this entreaty, the priest asks them to put away their distractions, to center their thoughts for the next few minutes, at least, on the Mass. And may the people make a vigorous effort! May it never be said of us, "this people honoreth me with their lips: but their heart is far from me" (Matt. 15:8).

Thoughts During the Preface

"Let us give thanks to the Lord," says the celebrant bowing; the people answer, "It is meet and just". And the priest repeats these words before he enlarges on them and the need of giving thanks. Read the *Preface* in your prayerbook. Surely it is meet and just and right to thank God. Christ before instituting the Eucharist at the Last Supper "gave thanks" to the Father (Luke 22:17; Matt. 26:27). Simply recall all the innumerable favors we have received from God: creation, our faith, the Mass, Christ, the saints—everything that we have is from

Him, and so we should give thanks for it all. To give thanks is to show appreciation. To give thanks sincerely is to learn to use the gifts correctly. Gratitude for favors received is the surest means of obtaining yet further benefits. An ungrateful person has few friends, and the *Preface* is a sharp reminder of our frequent ingratitude and calls us to give thanks at every moment.

The *Preface* usually contains some reference to the feast being celebrated, or to the season of the year (as Lent), or of the Mass itself (as in the Requiem). These references are, as a rule, brief, but very meaningful and elegant and help paint the occasion of our prayer in context with Christ's redemptive Passion. In these references, a short explanation of the feast or season is given, thus prompting us to give special thanks.

Ends in Hymn of Praise

Naturally, such a sublime hymn of praise and thanks should culminate in a thrilling, stirring chorus of praise and thanks of the angels. Each Preface, though different, all ends the same: in a jubilant, angelic cry of adoration. We add our voices to those of the heavenly choir:

> Holy! Holy! Holy! Lord God of hosts!
> Heaven and earth are full of Thy glory;
> Hosanna in the highest! Blessed is He
> That cometh in the name of the Lord.

The first part of this canticle is taken from a vision of the prophet Isaiah, from Isaiah 6:3. St. John likewise saw four living creatures round the throne crying, "Holy! Holy! Holy! Lord God, etc." (Apocalypse 4:6).

"*Hosanna*" is a Hebrew word which has remained untranslated so that we may be the more impressed, as it is a word so deeply rich. It is a cry of hope and yearning, a cry of loyalty and love combined, all tied together in the plea, "Save us, save us now!" "The multitude that went before and that followed cried saying: Hosanna to the Son of David: blessed is he that cometh in the name of the Lord" (Matt. 21:9). A need for saving, a definite hope of receiving it, a pledge of fidelity, and a sign of love are all tied together in this one word that we repeat thrice: *Hosanna*!

For each "Sanctus" that is said, the server rings the bell once. The bells are symbols to call in good and ward off evil, as found in the prayers for the baptism of bells in the Roman Ritual. The ringing of the bell signifies that grace is coming to both bring in Christ into our hearts and expel evil from those same hearts by the graces flowing through Holy Mother Church. The bells help call our attention to some important moment—whether the beginning of Mass, the removing of the chalice veil in some places, the beginning of the Canon, the final blessing of the hosts before the consecration, the Elevations, and the *Domine non sum dignus*—that grace is entering into this very temple of God in a real sacramental way that we can participate in.

Isn't the *Preface* a tingling, thrilling song? What is more natural than to sing, and sing aloud, when we recount the manifold gifts of God! At least, say the *Preface* and *Sanctus* quietly but fervently in your heart and soul, if it is not a Sung Mass and you cannot raise your voice with the choir's. Follow your Missal, and let this cry of adoration guide you through the Holy of Holies of the Roman Liturgy: the Canon of the Mass.

Questions for Discussion

1. What is the purpose of the Consecration?
2. What is the reason for the *Preface?*
3. Explain the opening dialogue. What should these several dialogues in the Mass (e. g., Dominus Vobiscum) mean to the people? Should they be interested?
4. Explain Matthew 15:8.
5. Show how the Mass is a sacrifice of thanksgiving.
6. Explain the *Sanctus.*
7. Read Isaias 6. Read Matthew 21:9.
8. Should the people sing at Mass? Why?

CANON

Prayers for the Church

We are at the *Canon* of the Mass, that is, the fixed, the stable, the unchanging part of the Mass. "Canon" is Greek for "rule, law, fixed order, standard." The *Canon* begins after the *Sanctus,* and ends at the *Pater Noster* (Our Father) when the *Communion* begins.

The Canon of the Mass is said silently by the celebrant. His face is not seen, his voice is not heard. He converses with the Great God in silence. This is to impress the congregation with the awe, the dread, the sacredness of the time. Something extraordinary, something stupendous, something utterly marvelous is happening. The silence emphasizes the fact that the celebrant is the minister of Christ, His spokesman, and the representative of the people. Like Moses on the Mount of Sinai, he is alone with God, pleading for his people. At a Solemn Mass, the incense, the bells, the torch-bearers remind us of the thunder, lightning, thick cloud, and horn blasts that shook the people with fear at the awesome majesty of God when Moses ascended the holy mountain of God to receive instructions from the Almighty (Exodus 19:16–19). Yet, the silence—so reminiscent of the quiet air where Elijah heard the voice of the Lord (3 Kings 19:13)—arouses devotion and recollection. These are precious moments—and too fleeting; they must not be lost in unnecessary business. The silence is our tribute of reverence to the mystery, our contribution to the hallowed nature of the present.

After the *Sanctus* the priest lifts up his eyes, raises his hands heavenward, joins them, and bowing profoundly, his hands resting on the altar, says the *Te Igitur*:

> We therefore humbly pray and beseech Thee (Te igitur), most merciful Father, through Jesus Christ Thy Son, Our Lord, that Thou wouldst accept and bless these † gifts, these † presents, these † holy unspotted sacrifices, which, in the first place, we offer Thee for Thy holy Catholic Church, which vouchsafe to pacify, guard, unite and govern throughout the whole world, together with Thy servant N., our Pope, N., our bishop, as also all orthodox believers and professors of the Catholic and Apostolic Faith.

After the *Preface* in which we addressed the Father and thanked Him most sincerely for all gifts, we feel we may now humbly beg new favors. We ask Him to bless these gifts and presents. The priest makes three signs of the cross over the gifts of bread and wine. They are our offerings; they stand for us, our unworthy selves. We beg God not to refuse them imperfect as they are and coming from such unworthy servants, and to make them resplendent with grace, as we too ask to be.

The sign of the Cross is made over them to bless them and to express all blessings come from the Cross and the Trinity's lavish bestowing of grace, the participation in the divine life. Just like us, these gifts of bread and wine will become pleasing only through their union with the sacrifice of the Cross.

We pray first for the whole Church. The Mass is Catholic, and it is of the Church as a whole that we ought first to think, before ourselves. We are members of the mystical body of Christ, recall; and in praying for all, we pray for ourselves—we are to love our neighbor like ourselves. We pray for peace. How timely is this petition! We have a very uncertain peace at present. Everyone fears tomorrow with its sure war. May it not happen, O Lord! The Mass teaches us peace, and asks for it every day at every altar. From now on, notice the several prayers for peace. The Mass obtains peace for us if we are of good will. When we are at peace, and everyone is at peace with himself, then universal peace must result, the so dearly sought and asked-for peace of Christ.

We pray also for unity. Have you ever read that paternal and touching prayer for unity, which Christ said after the Last Supper? If not, do so right now. "That they all may be one, as Thou, Father in me, and I in thee; that they also may be one in us; that the world may believe that thou hast sent me" (John 17:21).

We pray for our pope and for our bishop. They need our frequent prayers. Consider their numerous difficulties and their great burden to be the rulers of the Church. The "N" in the prayer-book stands for *name*. At the "N" put in the name of the pope, or the bishop and pray for him, that he may be made a holy ruler and eventually become a saint.

We must say these prayers with sincerity and not simply follow with our eyes, but turn these prayers into our own in our hearts. We must *pray* the Mass alongside the priest.

QUESTIONS FOR DISCUSSION

1. Why is the *Canon* of the Mass said silently?
2. Why are the gifts of bread and wine blessed with the Sign of the Cross at this time?
3. What is meant by peace and unity? Could you give the number of times the celebrant prays for peace during Mass?
4. How can peace only be obtained? Read St. Luke 2:14.
5. What do the "N's" mean? What is your bishop's name? What is his greatest need at the moment?

Remembrance of the Living

The celebrant bowed, and hands joined, now prays, "be mindful, O Lord, of Thy servants and handmaids N. and N." Here at "N" he mentions silently, or thinks of the names of the living for whom he wishes to pray. He mentions by name, for example, his parents, relatives, the sick and the dying, the poor, sinners, benefactors, friends, good works, the missions, the parish, and the like. At N. and N. the people are to mention in their mind, mentally, the names of those for whom they wish to pray. They may add any number of names and intentions. The laity also at this time should pray for the living. This is your sacrifice as well as the priest's—put the names of those for whom you wish to pray on the paten, in the chalice, and unite them to Christ's Sacrifice of infinite worth, that those for whom you intercede may receive more grace than is imaginable through this Holy Sacrifice of the Mass. It is not limited to simply one person. The laity should bring all of their needs at this moment—let them not forget their pastor and all priests and religious. Pray for all Catholic endeavors—the press, schools, hospitals—whatever the work, it will be blessed all the more by being added to the merits of the Cross.

Memento at the Mass

The good believing parishioners often ask a priest to remember them in the Mass, to give them a "memento." These people believe in the power of the Mass. The priest is very happy to give them a mention at this time: the remembrance of the living. The good thief asked of the dying Savior, "Remember me, Lord, when Thou shalt come into Thy kingdom" (Luke 23:42). And the Lord did remember him. To ask for a remembrance, a memento, is to ask for a prayer. To be remembered in one's prayer is the best of remembrances.

Then the celebrant prays for "all here present, whose faith and devotion are known unto Thee, for whom we offer, or who offer up to Thee this sacrifice of praise." Those who contribute to the support of the Church; those who give toward the Mass its requirements as wine, candles, vestments, altar decorations, etc., are prayed for especially. They are closely associated with the sacrifice. They benefit more than they who give almost nothing. Of course, they who gave the offering or stipend for this Mass benefit very specially. They receive the priest's special intention. The prayer warns us to have devotion and faith, "whose faith and devotion are known unto Thee." How can we be so disinterested at Mass, so careless, so unmindful? They who "offer up," they who participate in the Mass, they who unite themselves with the priest and Christ as victims and priests benefit abundantly. They appreciate the Mass.

The prayer includes "their families and friends." We ask God to remember those dear to us, in whom we are much interested. Does not the Church ask us to pray for parents, children, relatives, friends? The Church gives the example of praying "for the redemption of their souls, for the health and salvation they hope for." The Mass is a most plentiful source of grace. It is one of Calvary's channels, in fact, the primary channel, as it is the Prayer of Christ. The Mass is a sacrifice of atonement, of reparation—of redemption. It remits venial sins if one is sorry; it remits mortal sins indirectly by moving sinners to repentance. We are able to shorten Purgatory by attending Mass while on earth. We pray for health—for both spiritual and bodily health. Isn't this prayer something grand! All the beauty and all the richness in the Mass which is so often left buried and neglected! We are really rich, but poor on account of neglect. We have a treasury of the finest gold to draw from daily, but how often do we neglect merely open this vault's door!

"Who now pay their vows to Thee, etc." Those who now pay their homage to Thee, who fulfill now their resolutions, their promises, their obligations of religion to Thee. The Mass is a sacrifice of praise, thanks, petition and reparation. We intend through it to pay our debts of religion, of worship, to the Almighty.

How to Pray

Go to Mass daily, if at all possible. They who attend Mass benefit more than they who are absent. Give to your church and to the requirements of the Mass and you benefit still more. Have Masses said and the benefit is still greater. Follow the Mass with a Mass prayer-book, a Missal, and this grows it more, for this helps and intensifies your devotion. It makes you more attentive to following the Mass, with all of its prayers and rituals. Think about the marvelous prayers of the Mass—that will give you a love for the Mass. We do not love what we do not know, and the more we know something or someone who is so lovable, the greater our capacity for love is stretched by this knowledge of goodness.

Be in grace when you go to Mass and your fruits will be more abundant. If you cannot confess before Mass, at least make a good act of contrition, if there be mortal sin. Pray at Mass for the graces to renounce sin and to live a more holy life.

And if you can't go to Mass, if you can't be present, make the offering at home and unite yourself by intention to all the Masses happening in the world on on this day. This should be done every morning and recalled occasionally during the day. Remember the Mass is for all, even for the absent. The absent, however, do not profit as much as they who attend. "O Lord, I wish to offer you all the Masses of this day" you may say, "I wish to take part in them as much as I can." Isn't it worth while to receive a share in thousands of Masses daily, annually, as much as we can in our lifetimes?

Questions for Discussion

1. What action should the people do at this remembrance?
2. Can you, from this prayer, give a reason why one should attend Mass?
3. Can you tell, from this prayer, why one should contribute to the support of the Church?
4. Can you tell, from this prayer, in what order people benefit from the Mass?
5. For whom and for what does the Church pray for in this prayer from the *Sanctus* to the *Communicantes?*
6. Explain: "Whose faith and devotion are known to Thee".

The Communicantes
(In Communion With)

We have remembered the living on earth; we shall, after the Consecration, pray for the souls in Purgatory. Now—and what is more fitting?—we remember the saints in Heaven. The Church is composed of three sections: the Church militant (on earth), the Church suffering (in Purgatory), and the Church triumphant (in Heaven). The Mass is for all the Church. It is the sacrifice of the Mystical Body of Christ, no matter the member's location. Mindful of this too-little-appreciated teaching, we wish to honor the saints, in fact, we belong to the Communion of Saints. We pray to the saints in heaven and they pray for us. We wish to honor them upon earth by declaring their virtues; we wish to praise them. Above all, we do want to imitate their heroic lives—that is the best honor we can give them.

Therefore we pray: "We offer to Thee, O Lord, this Sacrifice of praise in union with and honoring in the first place the memory of the glorious ever Virgin Mary, Mother of our Lord and God, Jesus Christ..." It is proper that the Virgin should be mentioned first. She is the Queen of the Saints, the co-redemptrix and mediatrix of all graces. She cooperated so closely with her Son in the work of Redemption, she united herself so perfectly as a human person can to His Passion. that it would unfitting not to include her and she may not be omitted in the Mass.

After the Blessed Virgin, St. Joseph is mentioned, added to the Canon of the Mass by Pope St. John XXIII. St. Joseph is the greatest of all saints after Our Lady, due to his role as Spouse of the Blessed Virgin, appointed father to the Christ

Child, and universal patron of the Church. To St. Joseph is given proto-dulia, "first honor," among all the saints, and his insertion into the Canon is for this reason.

Then are mentioned the twelve Apostles, the Church's fulfilment of the twelve tribes of Israel. St. Paul is mentioned in the place of St. Matthias, who was chosen to fill the traitor's place. Next come for honorable mention twelve martyrs: five of whom were popes, one a bishop, one a deacon and five laymen. The Church, in her wisdom, has chosen saints from all walks of life to include in the holiest part of the Mass: all can enter, provided they live as best as they can as an *alter Christus*, another Christ. All these saints either lived or suffered in Rome, or, at least, were buried there, and thus became objects of special veneration on the part of the Church in Rome. Linus, Cletus and Clement were the immediate successors of St. Peter. Xystus, or Sixtus II, was pope from 257–258. Cornelius was the twentieth pope. He was martyred in 252. Cyprian, a convert, became bishop of Carthage in Africa, and was martyred in 258. He is a very noted church-writer. Laurence, an archdeacon, is better known. He was slowly roasted to death on a gridiron in 258.

Chrysogonus, a lay-teacher, was martyred in 304. John and Paul, brothers, had great wealth which they distributed in charity. They were beheaded in 362. Cosmos and Damian, also brothers, were doctors of great renown. They were martyred in Cilicia, Asia Minor, in 297. They are the patron saints of doctors and of medicine.

The prayer concludes, "and of all Thy saints, to whose merits and prayers do Thou grant that in all things we be protected, guarded, helped by Thee, through Christ our Lord. Amen."

Do we not feel much stronger and more confident after this prayer? We are in the company of the elect; we belong to the Communion of Saints. We honor; we praise; we pray to them. We are sure they will help us. They became saints through Christ and His grace, through the Mass and Holy Communion. May they help us especially in an appreciation and love for the Mass. We shall prove our honor for them by imitating them.

On five great feast-days—Christmas, Epiphany, Easter, Ascension and Pentecost—to this prayer is added a reference to the feast, or to the season. On Ascension, for example, we say, "In Communion with and celebrating this most holy day, whereon our Lord, Thy Sole-Begotten Son, set down at the right hand of Thy Glory the substance of our fraility united to Himself; and also we honor the memory first of, etc." You will find these references with their corresponding *Prefaces*, that is, before the *Canon*. These feasts add a special light to the work of Redemption that the Church has found it fitting to allow this feast's grandeur to frame ever so slightly the Canon for the priest as he prays.

QUESTIONS FOR DISCUSSION

1. Why do we mention the saints in this prayer?
2. Could you explain what is meant by saying the Blessed Virgin is Co-redemptrix and Mediatrix of all graces?
3. Tell something about each of the saints mentioned.
4. How do we honor the saints best?

Prayers before the Consecration

Shortly before the *Consecration* we are notified that the most solemn part of the Mass approaches. The server sounds the bell to notify the people, as the celebrant extends his hands over the offering and says:

"We, therefore, beseech Thee, O Lord, graciously to accept this oblation of our servitude, as also of Thy whole family; and to dispose our days in Thy peace, preserve us from eternal damnation, and rank us in the number of Thine elect. Through Christ Our Lord. Amen."

MEANING OF EXTENDED HANDS

This extending of the celebrant's hands over the chalice (and host) has important significance. This was done in the Old Testament by the priest to express the handing over, the transference of the people's sins to the victim. "He offered also the calf for sin: and when Aaron and his sons had put their hands upon the head thereof, He immolated it" (Leviticus 8:15). At the ordination of priests, the bishop places his hands on the candidates to express the giving of sacerdotal power, and one hand for the giving of the diaconate to deacons. Also, at confirmation the bishop extends his hands over the candidates to express the giving of the Holy Ghost. Here in the Mass, the priest uses the same gesture to express the transference of sins from ourselves to the victim. This gesture also expresses our identification, our oneness, with the victim.

THE VICTIM OFFERED

Through our sins we are guilty of death. Our lives should be taken away for having misused our faculties and gifts in sinning against the Giver of life, God. We are traitors and rebels; therefore, death is our due. But God does not wish our death; He gives us a substitute who will die for us. We transfer our sins to this victim. God would not allow Abraham to sacrifice his son Isaac, but sent him a "ram amongst the briars sticking fast by the horns which he took and offered for a holocaust instead of his son" (Genesis 22:13). Ever since then, in the Old Testament, animal sacrifice took the place of the offering of the beloved son by the man faithful to the Most High. In the Mass, this section expresses the fact that our sins are remitted on account of Christ's death. "How much more shall the blood of Christ, who by the Holy Ghost offered Himself unspotted unto God, cleanse our conscience from dead work to serve the living God? He is the mediator of the new testament" (Hebrews 9:14).

In this prayer we ask God to accept these offerings as a sign of our interior sacrifice—life, service, good-will, etc. It is the sacrifice of us all, the whole Church, especially of those who are sharing in and co-offering this Mass. We know the Mass is pleasing to God, but we fear and hesitate lest we, poor, miserable traitors, may make It less pleasing, hence we ask for the grace to purify our faults and to make ours as perfectly united to Christ as possible.

We ask God to grant us peace; preserve us from the everlasting flames of Hell; that we be numbered among the saved in Heaven. We ask God to give us the necessary graces to persevere, or, more correctly, to help us cooperate with the graces He necessarily gives; "Wherefore, brethren, labor the more, that by good works you may make sure your calling and election. For doing these things, you shall not sin at any time" (2 Peter 1:10).

Last Prayer before the Consecration

In this prayer, for the last time the celebrant begs God to look with favor on these gifts. The priest declares again and again that he is unworthy to present this most august Sacrifice and he begs God to overlook his unworthiness and to regard only His Son. The priest expresses several times his sorrow and humility, for he knows this Sacrifice is acceptable only in proportion to his repentance. May, therefore, this Sacrifice be acceptable since we are so very contrite!

"Which oblation do Thou, O God, we beseech Thee, vouchsafe to make in all things blessed †, approved †, reasonable and acceptable; that it may become for us the Body † and Blood † of Thy most beloved Son, Our Lord Jesus Christ."

At each † the priest makes the sign of the Cross. This reminds him that the Mass is the continued renewal of the death of Christ on Calvary. This Sacrifice is so powerful on account of His sacrifice on the Cross. The identity of the Mass and Calvary is noticed in the sixteen signs of the Cross which the priest makes on himself and the twenty-nine which he makes over the gifts.

We beg God that through the Mass we may be blessed. These gifts will be blessed as no other thing is blessed: Transubstantiation.

"Make it approved." We ask Him to approve it—that it be not rejected on account of being untrue, that is, when there is a lack of harmony or correspondence between the exterior gifts and interior heart and spirit; between the words and the spirit.

"Make it ratified," that is, a true and valid offering. It is a formal request for consecration. The celebrant solemnly implores the divine intervention that the lowly elements or bread and wine may become the hallowed Host. If the gifts are blessed and approved, they will be ratified.

"Make it reasonable and acceptable." The Mass is a sacrifice most reasonable—according to reason—for it is the sacrifice of

a living Person, a human-divine Person, the Son of God. "For it is impossible that with the blood of oxen and goats sin should be taken away. Then said I: Behold I come: in the head of the book it is written of me: that I should do thy will, O God. In the which will, we are sanctified by the oblation of the body of Jesus Christ once" (Hebrews, 10:4–10).

Our sacrifice is reasonable and acceptable when there is an interior sacrifice, and not simply empty, meaningless, insincere external signs. "I beseech you, brethren, by the mercy of God, that you present your bodies a living sacrifice, holy, pleasing unto God, your reasonable service" (Romans 12:1). How do we present our bodies a living, sincere, interior sacrifice? Let the tongue speak kind and honest words; let the ears hearken only to truth and good; let the hands give in help and not in anger; let the mind dwell on wholesome subjects; let us seek first the kingdom of God and His justice.

Listen to what St. Augustine says about Christian sacrifice and the human body. "Thus a true sacrifice is every work which is done that we may be united to God in holy fellowship. Man himself, consecrated and vowed to God, is a sacrifice in so far as he dies to the world that he may live to God . . . If then, the body, which, being inferior, the soul uses as a servant or instrument, is a sacrifice when it is used rightly, and with reference to God, how much more does the soul itself become a sacrifice when it offers itself to God in order that, being inflamed by the fire of this love, it may receive His beauty and become pleasing to Him, losing the shape of earthly desire" (*City of God, X, 7*).

QUESTIONS FOR DISCUSSION

1. Why does the celebrant extend his hands over the chalice?
2. Explain fully this prayer.
3. Explain: "make in all things approved, blessed, reasonable".
4. When is our sacrifice reasonable and acceptable?

5. What is meant by the *Consecration?*
6. What should the people do during the *Elevation?*

The Consecrations and Elevations

As this is the most tender of moments, and should be the most intimate with Our Savior—only second to receiving Holy Communion and the union that comes with that—this should be when prayer takes the most personal elements. When Jesus Christ Himself comes down before our eyes, let your very person speak to Him. Various aspirations can be said: "My Lord and My God," "Truly, this is the Son of God," "Lord, I believe, help my unbelief," "May the blood of Jesus flow down upon me and cleanse me," etc.

Whatever the prayer may be, the most important thing is that it be true prayer.

Prayers after the Consecration

The Victim, Jesus Christ, is lying on the altar. The Consecration made Christ present as Victim of this sacrifice under the appearances of bread and wine. We now present in words our sacrifice to the Father. By the very fact that Christ is present through the *Consecration,* he is offered as a Victim to God. Sacrifice and offering include each other. In the very act in which the Victim is sacrificed, it is likewise offered to God. The rendering present of the Victim carries with it the expression of sacrifice—obedience, humility, contrition, conformity to the will of God, etc.

We need, however, to express exteriorly, in words and in actions, our mind. Even though the offering of the Victim is already contained in the sacrificial action; nevertheless, we wish to give audible and group expression of our offering to Heaven:

> Wherefore, O Lord, we Thy servants, and likewise Thy holy people, calling to mind the blessed Passion of Thy Son, together with His Resurrection and Ascension, offer unto Thy excellent Majesty, of Thy gifts and presents, a pure † Victim, a holy † Victim, an immaculate † Victim: The holy † bread of eternal life and the chalice † of everlasting salvation.

At the sign of the †, the priest makes a Sign of the Cross over the Species (bread and wine). These signs do not bless but declare the relation between the Mass and the cross. In these words we give our Gift to the Father. This gift is His Son. This Gift is Christ and we know God is pleased with us for we are united with the Son in whom He is well pleased. Christ on the Cross—and all His life—presented to the Father His obedience, charity, penance, etc. This offering is repeated at every Mass for Calvary, the one, grand expression of Christ's sacrifice, is renewed.

In the Mass, we also remember His Passion. For the Mass has worth only through His Passion and death. The Mass distributes and applies what His passion merited. We also recall the Resurrection and Ascension, for these two miracles were the Father's stamp of approval on His Son's life and work.

Since the Mass is performed repeatedly in time by human ministers, we ask God to look as favorably upon It as He did on the sacrifices of Abel, Abraham, and Melchisedech. Abel offered the best lamb of his flock. St. Paul says that by faith he "offered to God a sacrifice exceeding that of Cain, by which God gave him a testimony that he was just" (Hebrews 11:4).

Abraham was told to sacrifice his son, Isaac. "Take thy son and sacrifice him on the mountain I will show thee." Abraham proceeded to obey. All was ready for the slaying of Isaac when God stayed Abraham's uplifted hand; God wanted only the obedience, the readiness, the resignation of Abraham. He was pleased with the gesture (Genesis 14:18). This willingness to give up the greatest good he had in the world was most pleasing to God so that it became the prototype for the Chosen People of what sacrifice was to be.

Melchisedech was a king and priest. He is one of the best types or figures of Christ in the Old Testament, for he offered a sacrifice of bread and wine. "Thou art a priest forever according to the order of Melchisedech" (Hebrews 7:17). Hence we have the words of the Missal:

> "Upon which do Thou vouchsafe to look with favorable and gracious countenance, and accept them, as Thou wast pleased to accept the gifts of Thy just servant Abel, and the sacrifice of our Patriarch Abraham, and that of Thy Highpriest Melchisedech."

Third Prayer after the Consecration

Bowing profoundly before the altar, to show his humility, the celebrant says the prayer:

> We humbly beseech Thee, Almighty God, command these to be carried by the hands of Thy holy Angel to Thine Altar on high, in the presence of Thy divine Majesty, that as many as shall, by partaking at this Altar, receive the most sacred Body and Blood of Thy Son, may be filled with all heavenly blessing and grace, through the same Christ Our Lord. Amen.

Who is this "holy Angel" who carries our offering to God? Some say it is Saint Michael, the prince of the heavenly hosts and guardian of the Church on earth. Others say it is the patron of that particular church or chapel in which the Mass is said. We prefer to consider this "holy Angel" as Christ Himself. "Angel" means "messenger", or rather, "ambassador". The Son of God was, as He said Himself, sent by His Father. He is the Angel par excellence; He is the Angel of the Great Council. He is our one, great Mediator. Regardless of precisely who this angel is, let us call to mind that angels surround us at Mass, and let us pray to them, as the saints, for help in worshipping God in the most perfect way that we can.

MEANING OF PRAYER

"To Thine sublime Altar on high, in the presence of Thy divine Majesty." There can be no question of a physical taking up to heaven of the consecrated elements, nor is there a material altar set up in heaven. The Church uses these terms in a symbolical sense. The prayer refers to a scene which St. John gives in his Apocalypse or Book of Revelations. The Apostle saw these things in a vision on the island of Patmos. "And another angel came and stood before the altar, having a golden censer; . . . that he should offer of the prayers of all saints upon the golden altar, which is before the throne of God. And the smoke of the incense of the prayers of the saints ascended up before the throne of God from the hand of the Angel" (7:3). In chapter five and nine, there is yet another mention "of the golden altar, which is before the eyes of God." We should recall that the Book of Revelation is a glimpse at the eternal heavenly liturgy, the perpetual worship of God, which we are blessed to be able to truly participate in while on earth through the Holy Sacrifice of the Mass. This prayer recalls that we too are partakers in the eternal courts while still breathing, and that we are "in the presence of Thy divine Majesty," and that we should direct our prayers as such.

The prayer asks that the Body and Blood of Christ, as they are our Sacrifice, may be united to and offered with that eternal oblation of Himself by which Christ ratifies forever that actual oblation of Himself which took place but once upon the altar of the cross. The golden altar in heaven is but one more symbol by which the inspired writer, St. John, describes the office of Mediator which our good Savior discharges in our behalf.

Christ Our Sacrifice

In this prayer we ask God to accept our sacrifice as He accepts the eternal sacrifice of Christ. "For that He continueth forever hath an everlasting priesthood, whereby he is able also to save forever them that come to God by Him; always living to make intercession for us" (Hebrews 7:25). Our sacrifice is Christ; our gifts of self-sacrifice are joined with His. The two become one Sacrifice—His. And He presents it to the Father. That is why the Mass is the best Sacrifice; our gifts of bread and wine representing ourselves become Christ the Victim.

In the ordaining of a subdeacon, the bishop says the words: "The altar of holy Church is Christ Himself, according as St. John bears testimony when he relates in his Apocalypse how he saw a golden Altar, standing before the throne, on which and by which the offerings of the faithful are consecrated to God."

We finish this beautiful prayer with the request that all who partake at this altar by receiving communion may be filled with all heavenly blessing and grace. No wonder the priests constantly beg their people to receive the Body and Blood of Christ in Communion. They who receive participate more closely in the Mass; they receive more abundantly His graces and blessings. "He who eats my flesh and drinks my blood abides in me, and I in him" (John 6:57). We give to God ourselves through Christ; God returns Himself to us by Christ. Communion is a sharing in the Divinity. It is the eating of the heavenly Banquet.

QUESTIONS FOR DISCUSSION

1. What is the thought in these prayers?
2. Why is the Sign of the Cross made so frequently?
3. Who is the Gift we give to the Father? Why? How is this made possible?
4. Who was Abraham, Abel, Melchisedech? Read Genesis 4, 14, and 22.
5. Find out something about the Apocalypse.
6. Who is "Thy holy Angel" mentioned here?
7. Read the admirable *Encyclical* "ON THE HOLY EUCHARIST" by Leo XIII.

Remembrance of the Dead

At this time, in our charity, we pray for the souls in Purgatory. They cannot help themselves, but look to us for aid. "Remember me, at least you, my friends." The Mass is a sacrifice of reparation and propitiation; it is the greatest help to the suffering souls. "It is a holy and wholesome thought to pray for the dead, that they may be loosed from their sins" (2 Maccabees 12:46).

> Remember also, O Lord, Thy servants and handmaids, N. and N., who have gone before us with the sign of faith, and sleep the sleep of peace.

At N. and N., the celebrant mentions those for whom he wishes to pray particularly. And the people should pray for those whom they know or know of who have gone before them—parents, relatives, friends, priests, teachers, members of the parish, the most forgotten souls, the ones closest to Heaven, etc., etc. Pray for those who are suffering on our account—who sinned on account of us. Pray for the Poor Souls. Some day we shall be one of them and we shall be happy to have some of the present Poor Souls praying for us in Heaven. Do not depend too much on the living praying for you after death.

The Church prays for all the souls in Purgatory even those not mentioned by name:

> "To these, and to all who rest in Christ, grant, a place of refreshment, of light, and of peace. Through Christ Our Lord. Amen."

The Church gives the example of charity. As the prayers of the Church are for all, so should our prayers be for all. Pray even for those—especially those—in Purgatory whom you disliked on earth.

We do not know how long souls must suffer in Purgatory. Pray for them all your years. And have Masses said for them. As we already mentioned, do not depend on the help you get from earth after your death. When you are in Purgatory, the saints whom you helped to Heaven will remember you.

St. Monica told her son, St. Augustine, "Lay this body anywhere; let not the care for that in any way disquiet you: this only I request, that you would remember me at the Lord's altar whereever you be."

Up to Us Sinners

It is only natural that we think of ourselves, we the living, after having remembered the dead. Some day soon we shall be with the departed in the prison house of eternal justice, whence there is no escape until full payment has been made, even to the last farthing (Matt. 5:26).

"To us also, Thy sinful servants, who hope in the multitude of Thy mercies vouchsafe to grant some part and fellowship with Thy holy Apostles and martyrs, etc." At the first words which are said somewhat aloud in order to draw the attention the priest strikes his breast. This is in imitation of the humble publican, who, standing afar off, would not so much as lift up his eyes towards heaven, but struck his breast, saying, "O God, be merciful to me a sinner" (Luke 18:13).

A necessary condition for forgiveness is humility, to acknowledge sincerely our guilt. "God resisteth the proud, but to the humble He giveth His grace" (James 4:6). This prayer recalls the Confiteor. We publicly acknowledge that we are sinners. It is good to do so at this time, for we have seen in the prayers what wonderful blessings and gifts are ours in the Mass. We must not now become proud. "The prayer of him that humbleth himself shall pierce the clouds" (Eccl. 25:21). It is a laudable custom, so says Fr. Nicholas Gihr in his magnificent work on the Holy Mass, to strike one's breast with the priest here. "Nobis quoque peccatoribus" is the only phrase spoken aloud in the entire Canon—clearly, Holy Mother Church wishes us to be particularly attentive to this phrase. We are sinners, but we also are God's servants—for that reason, we have great hope to be admitted into the court of His saints through His mercy. We plea for mercy, confess our guilt, and pray for sainthood by this striking of our breast.

We pray to become saints, enter Heaven, and have fellowship with the saints. Now follows the mention of fifteen saints, all of whom are martyrs. This list supplements the one given before the *Consecration*. We mention first St. John the Baptist, the precursor of Christ, the preacher and model of penance.

Then St. Stephen, the first martyr after the Resurrection, one of the seven deacons appointed by the Apostles, "a man full of faith and the Holy Ghost" (Acts 6:5). St. Matthias took the place of Judas among the Apostles. Barnabas was one of the seventy-two disciples, "a good man, and full of the Holy Ghost and of faith" (Acts 11:24). He was for a time a companion of St. Paul.

St. Ignatius was the second successor of St. Peter as bishop of Antioch. A legend says St. Ignatius was the child whom Our Lord placed in the midst of the Apostles as a model of humility and simplicity (Matt. 18). He was martyred in 107 in Rome. St. Alexander was the fifth successor of St. Peter as Pope. He was beheaded in 115. St. Marcellinus was a priest in Rome, and St. Peter an exorcist. They were beheaded about the year 300.

Saints Felicity and Perpetua were two women, the latter a noblewoman and the former a slave. They were beheaded at Carthage in Africa in 202. St. Agatha, a virgin, was martyred in Sicily, 251. St. Lucy is another of Sicily's martyr-virgins. She was denounced to the pagan judges by the young man to whom her parents had bethrothed her. She was beheaded in 304. St. Agnes suffered martyrdom in her thirteenth year, 304. St. Cecilia, a noble virgin of Rome, was married to Valerian only after the Lord assured her that she could remain faithful to her vow of virginity. She was martyred in 177. St. Anastasia was a noble widow of Rome and was martyred Dec. 25, 304. Again, similar to the prayer before the Consecrations, the Church paints a picture of the Church triumphant, and we see that all people from all walks of life—saints from the Old Covenant and the New, noble and slave, man and woman, bishop and layman. All can become saints and join in the heavenly court.

With these and all the Saints, we beg to have companionship, "into whose company we beseech Thee to admit us not weighing our merits, but pardoning our offenses."

QUESTIONS FOR DISCUSSION

1. Why do some souls go to Purgatory?
2. Why should we help the Poor Souls?
3. Does the Mass help the Poor Souls?
4. Do indulgences help them?
5. Can you explain indulgences? How are they gained?

Last Prayers after the Consecration

This section of the Mass called the *Consecration* is concluded with an extraordinary summarizing prayer:

Through whom, O Lord, Thou dost always create, sanctify, † vivify, † bless and give unto all these goods things. By Him, and with Him, and in Him is to Thee, God, Almighty Father, in the unity of the Holy Ghost, all honor and glory, world without end. Amen.

It will help us to understand this prayer if we remember that years and years ago at this part of the Mass, the people brought to the altar bread, wine, fruit, vegetables, and the like to be blessed. This custom gradually disappeared due to the increase in the number of Masses. Today, a reminder of this old practice is to be seen on Holy Thursday when the bishop blesses the Holy Oils at this part of the Mass.

We may say that now "all these goods things" means the Sacred Species. By the Consecration, bread and wine have been "sanctified," that is, set apart and made holy; they have been "vivified," that is, changed into the living and life-giving Body and Blood of Christ; they have been "blessed" indeed, that is, they are filled with best of blessings for us. The celebrant, at †, makes a Sign of the Cross over the Species to denote the relation between the Mass and Calvary.

THE MINOR ELEVATION

The priest now uncovers the chalice, genuflects, rises and taking the Sacred Host in his right hand, holds it over the Chalice and traces three Crosses with It; then he makes two Crosses between the Chalice and himself. Finally he raises a bit both the Chalice and the Host while he says "all honor and glory." This is the "minor elevation." He places the Host on the corporal, covers the Chalice, and genuflects. During this eloquent ceremony, he says, "through Him, and with Him, and in Him is to Thee Almighty God, Father, in unity with the Holy Ghost, all honor and glory."

The Sign of the Cross is made with the Host over the Chalice to indicate that in it is the Precious Blood of Christ whose Body is the Host. The Sign of the Cross at the name of the "Father" and "Holy Ghost" is not made over the Chalice but outside it—between it and the priest—for neither the Father nor the Holy Ghost is sacrificed.

At the "minor elevation" we should with all sincerity say "all honor and glory." This last elevation is the last ceremony in which we declare to God our praise. Always remember, we go to God by way of Christ—"through Him, and by Him and with Him and in Him." Christ is the "Son in Whom I am well pleased." Our sacrifice and prayers have worth and value because they are joined with those of Christ. Of ourselves we are nothing, we are helpless and poor; but in Christ we are something, we are rich and strong. Christ is the head of His Mystical Body—the Church. He is the Vine, we are the branches.

QUESTIONS FOR DISCUSSION

1. Explain the *Nobis Quoque Peccatoribus*.
2. Tell something about the saints mentioned here.
3. Could you give a short talk on the necessity of humility?
4. What is the "little elevation" and its meaning?
5. Explain fully "Through Him, and by Him and with Him and in Him".
6. Explain the Signs of the Cross made here.

Communion

The Our Father

The Consecration ends and the *Communion* begins with the *Our Father*. The Communion is a partaking of the Sacrifice. It is eating of the Sacrifice. It is the Sacrifice-Banquet. St. Paul referred to Holy Communion as "eating the Sacrifice", "partaking of the Table of the Lord", and "eating the Lord's Supper" (1 Cor. 10:16, 21, and 11:23 sq.). In the Sacrifice we give to God; in the Sacrifice-Banquet, or Holy Communion, God gives to us—Himself. God is never outdone in generosity; He returns to us a hundredfold for every gift we make to Him.

In most sacrifices, the offerer ate the victim. This he did to express his wish to unite, to identify himself with the diety. In Holy Communion, we receive the Victim, Christ, to unite ourselves with Christ, to be like God in grace.

Before we sit down to a meal we say grace. We may consider the *Our Father* as grace before the Heavenly Banquet, Holy Communion. It is the table prayer—"Give us this day our daily bread." This petition is applied first to the needs of the spirit, and secondly to those of the body. This phrase also served as a reminder to the faithful that it was Our Lord's wish to see them come daily to partake of the "living Bread which came down from Heaven" (John 6:51).

The *Our Father* is a very suitable connecting-prayer, a transition prayer between the *Communion* and *Consecration*. The first three requests regard the honor and glory of God; the last three, the salvation of man. These two sections are linked by "give us this day our daily bread". In the *Consecration*, God is considered; in the Communion, man. In the *Communion*, God comes to man that man can go to God.

The *Our Father* is introduced with the short preface, "Let us pray. Instructed by Thy saving precepts and following Thy divine institution we dare to say". We make bold to address God as Father because Christ instructed us so to pray (Matt. 6:9).

During this divinely instituted prayer, the priest has his eyes fixed on the Sacred Host. This is in recognition of the giving of the Lord's prayer by Christ and of the command to pray in His name. It is hardly necessary to entreat that this prayer should be said with great earnestness, feeling, and deliberation. Likewise, our eyes should be fixed on God in preparation for receiving Him in Holy Communion. The *Our Father* is the perfect prayer, and thus it is the perfect preparation for Holy Communion.

"Our Father, who art in heaven, hallowed be Thy name. Thy kingdom come. Thy will be done, on earth as it is in Heaven. Give us this day our daily bread, and forgive us our trespasses as we forgive those who trespass against. And lead us not into temptation, but deliver us from evil. Amen."

The *Our Father* should be said with great earnestness and deliberation. If we ponder its various petitions, even superficially, we cannot fail to be struck with their singular beauty and dignity. This should by itself prevent any unseeming haste in their recitation.

St. Augustine on the Our Father

The Lord's Prayer has ever been the favorite prayer of Holy Church. The early Fathers and Doctors and the Saints of later centuries have left us commentaries upon this divine masterpiece, of which Tertullian says that the terseness of its wording is matched by its depth of meaning. It seems right to make a few comments upon the seven petitions of the divinely dictated prayer, but it is best to do so, not in one's own words, but in the weighty ones of a great Father of the Church.

One of the most admirable treatises upon prayer that have come down to us from the early centuries of Christianity is a letter of St. Augustine to a noble lady of the name of Proba. This lady had but recently become a widow and found herself at the head of a large household. She was still young and her wealth was immense, but realizing the vanity of all things earthly she felt but one desire, namely, to serve the Lord with all her heart. When Alaric plundered Rome, she narrowly escaped from the violence of his Goths. Fearing their return, she sold her possessions and went to live at Carthage with a number of maidens and young widows. She consulted the Bishop of Hippo about prayer: how ought she to pray and what should be the object of her supplication? Augustine's answer is a long and detailed exposition of the necessity and advantage of prayer. In chapter XI of the treatise he gives a brief analysis and explanation of the Lord's Prayer, clearly showing therein that, to his mind, it was the perfect prayer, expressing all our needs, and all the more powerful as it is not so much ours as Christ's, Who taught it to His disciples.

"To us," says the holy Doctor, "words are necessary, that by them we may be assisted in considering and observing what we ask, not as means by which we expect that God to be either informed or moved to compliance." When, therefore, we say: 'Hallowed be Thy name,' we admonish ourselves to desire that His name, which is always holy, may be also among men esteemed holy, that is to say, not despised; which is an advantage, not to God, but to men.

"When we say: 'Thy kingdom come,' which shall certainly come, whether we wish it or not, we do by these words stir up our own desires for that kingdom, that it may come to us, and that we may be found worthy to reign in it. When we say: 'Thy will be done on earth as it is in heaven,' we pray for ourselves, that He would give us the grace of obedience, that His will may be done by us in the same way as it is done in heavenly places by His Angels. When we say: 'Give us this day our daily bread,' the words 'this day' signifies for the present time, in which we ask either for that competency of temporal blessing which I have spoken of before ('bread' being used to designate the whole of those blessings, because of it constituting so important a part of them), or the Sacrament of believers, which is in this present time necessary, but necessary in order to obtain the felicity not of the present time, but of eternity.

"When we say: 'Forgive us our debts as we forgive our debtors,' we remind ourselves of both what we should ask and what we should do in order that we may be worthy to receive what we ask. When we say: 'Lead us not into temptation,' we admonish ourselves to seek that we may not, through being deprived of God's help, be either ensnared to consent or compelled to yield to temptation. When we say: 'Deliver us from evil,' we admonish ourselves to consider that we are not yet enjoying that good estate in which we shall experience no evil. This last petition, according to the holy Doctor, is so comprehensive that a Christian, in whatsoever affliction he be placed, 'may begin with this petition, go on with it, and with it conclude his prayers.'" (*Homiletic Review*, April, 1924).

The Empty Paten

In solemn Masses you have noticed the sub-deacon with the vellum over his shoulders standing on the floor of the sanctuary in the center. He is holding the empty paten, the saucer-like golden plate. In the first six centuries of the Church, it was on this plate that the hosts were collected and distributed to the people at Holy Communion. But when this custom ended, in order that the paten might not be in the way of the priest at the altar (for it was very large in former days), the sub-deacon would take care of it until it was needed again. During the *Our Father* it is brought to the altar again for it is to be used very soon to receive the Sacred Host.

Another explanation is sometimes given. In the first centuries, the sub-deacon held on the paten a small piece of the Sacred Host from the Mass of the previous day. At the entry of the officers of the Mass for the sacrifice, This was adored. A fraction of the Host was always kept for the next Mass when it was dropped into the Precious Blood. This expressed the unity of the Mass, linking every Sacrifice to the first instituted at the Last Supper.

Deliver Us, O Lord

The Mass-servers (and the people, too) join in the last petition by saying, "But deliver us from evil." This petition is paraphrased, developed by the priest in a lengthy prayer:

> "Deliver us, we beseech Thee, O Lord, from all evils, past, present and to come: and by the intercession of Mary ever Virgin, Mother of God, together with Thy Apostles Peter and Paul and Andrew, and all Thy Saints, graciously give peace in our days, that aided by the help of Thy mercy, we may be always free from sin and secure from all disturbance."

This prayer is most comprehensive and makes no distinction between physical and moral evils. When the Church prays to be delivered from past evils, she has in mind not only the sins by which some of her children have offended God, but likewise the consequences and punishments of these transgressions; for even though sin is blotted out by repentance, the temporal punishment due to sin is not thereby wholly removed. The effects of past sin often endure in the way of bad example, evil consequence for the mind and body, evil habits, etc.

We ask to be delivered from present evil. Evils are the results of original sin. The upset world is a strong argument for the fact of original sin, "Every creature groaneth and travaileth in pain, even till now. And not only it, but ourselves also, who have the first fruits of the spirit, waiting for the adoption of the sons of God, the redemption of our body" (Rom. 8:22).

What Is Peace

We pray, "grant peace in our day." How badly we need it! This petition was inserted in the Mass by Pope St. Gregory the Great, around 600. In his age, the times were very much disturbed by wars, famines, floods, invasions and barbarians. Many thought the end of the world was at hand. And some

now suspect the end of the world to be soon. The world is so disturbed and out-of-order. Peace is so much desired.

To have peace all around—personal, social and international—there must be no sin. "From whence come wars and contentions among you? Come they not hence, from your concupiscences which war in your members? You covet and have not, you kill and envy and cannot obtain. You contend and war" (James 4:1). Peace is the tranquility of order. When my soul is in order, my passions under control and God given the first place, I have peace. When everyone is at peace with himself, there results public peace. Notice how frequently the prayer for peace occurs in the Communion of the Mass. Peace is so necessary and something every man deeply desires.

As soon as the priest begins to say this prayer, "deliver us, O Lord, from evils, etc.," he wipes the paten with the purificator (a narrow piece of linen), takes it in his right hand, holds it erect upon the altar until he comes to the words, "give us peace in our days," when he makes the Sign of the Cross upon himself with it. This expresses that peace comes from the Cross. "In the Cross is life, salvation and freedom" (Galatians 6:6). It is also a prayer to share in the peace of the Cross. Then the paten is kissed as a token of respect, because the Host will now rest upon it.

Questions for Discussion

1. Why is the Lord's Prayer said here?
2. Explain it fully. Can we say it with true devotion when we hate or refuse to speak to our neighbor?
3. Explain why in a Solemn Mass the Subdeacon holds the paten in the veil.
4. Explain the prayer, "Deliver us O Lord", said after the *Our Father*.
5. What can you say about peace and its acquisition?

THE BREAKING OF THE HOST

While the priest says, "through the same Jesus Christ, Thy Son, Our Lord," he holds respectfully the Host over the Chalice, breaks it into halves and places the one he has in his right hand on the paten. From the half in his left hand he breaks off a small piece whilst he says, "who with Thee lives and reigns." This particle he holds in his right hand, while he places the part in his left beside the other half on the paten, meanwhile saying, "in the unity of the Holy Ghost, God." Holding the fragment over the chalice, he says or sings, "forever and ever." The server or choir respond, "Amen." The priest then makes three crosses with the fragment over the chalice saying, "the peace of the Lord be ever with you." The server answers "and with thy spirit." Then the celebrant drops the particle into the Precious Blood saying, "may this commingling and consecration of the Body and Blood of Our Lord Jesus Christ become to us, who receive It, effectual unto eternal life, Amen."

After Our Lord had Himself instituted the Mass at the Last Supper, He bade the Apostles do in their turn what they had just witnessed. "Jesus took bread, and blessed, and broke" (Matt. 26:26). The two disciples at Emmaus recognized Jesus for "He took bread, and blessed and broke and gave to them" (Luke 24:30). "To break bread" became the expression for the Mass in the early Church. "And continuing daily with one accord in the temple, and breaking bread from house to house" (Acts 2:46).

The breaking of the Host recalls events of both the Old and New Testaments. In the Jewish Pasch service, the bread was broken to symbolize the affliction of God's chosen people during their bondage in Egypt. Likewise, the breaking of the

Host reminds us of the death of the Savior on the Cross, the bruising of the wounded body of Christ. "He was wounded for our iniquities and bruised for our sins" (Isaias 53:5). When this rite was performed by Our Lord at the Last Supper, it heralded the violent sufferings of His Passion. "This is My Body broken for you." Oftentimes, we can hear the Host being fractured—let that call to mind the sufferings Our Lord endured during His sacred Passion.

The Host broken into three parts may be taken to express the three Persons in the Trinity who are present therein. The fraction may also express the three divisions of the Church, Christ's Mystical body: the militant, the suffering, the triumphant Church.

In the early centuries of the Church, the Host was rather large. Sections of it were broken off and sent by the pope or bishop to the bishops and pastors in and about Rome not present at that Mass. This ceremony aptly expressed their unity with the Church—that they were in communion with the Vicar of Christ, not excommunicated. We have already seen (after the *Our Father*) that a portion of the Host was reserved for the next Mass when it was dropped into the Chalice. This eloquently expressed the unity of the Mass with the Sacrifice on Calvary. Both sacrifices have the same Victim and Priest, only the manner of offering is different. "In a true sense there is but one Mass in all the world; and by inserting thus yesterday's Mass into today's and today's into tomorrow's, this unity was vigorously proclaimed" (Martindale, *The Mind of The Missal*).

The mingling of the consecrated elements, the Host and the Blood, expresses that Christ is whole and entire under each Species. Where His Blood is there also is His Body; where His Body is there also is His Blood. This mingling also expresses the Resurrection. As the separation of Body and Blood is represented by the separate consecration and by the breaking of the Host, so by the union of these elements the glorious Resurrection of Christ is pictured. Likewise, it reminds us of our own death. We shall have our bodies and souls separated, but on the Last Day, in the Resurrection of the Body, we too shall rise from the grips of death.

The Host is broken over the Chalice. It may be that this is done out of respect, so that any falling particles at the fraction may drop into the Chalice. It is so done also to show that the Body and Blood are of one and the same Victim, Christ.

The breaking of the Host is a preparation and introduction to the Holy Communion. Breaking the bread means a preparation for a meal; a getting-ready to eat. Now in the Mass, the Bread is broken for the Banquet, for the Sacrifice-Repast. Everyone present at the sacrifice should be ready to partake of It by way of communion.

Questions for Discussion

1. Explain the breaking of the Host and its accompanying prayer.
2. How is charity referred to here?
3. Show how the prayers and ceremonies from the *Our Father* prepare one for receiving Holy Communion.
4. What are the various meanings and symbolism in the breaking of the Host?

The Agnus Dei

The *Agnus Dei* is an admirable prayer in preparation for Holy Communion. In it we address Christ as the Lamb of God. John the Baptist called the Savior "the lamb of God who shall take away the sins of the world." In the Old Testament, the lamb was one of the ordinary victims offered as a sacrifice. The lamb is the animal of innocence, of meekness, of submission, and of willing sacrifice. It allows itself to be led to slaughter without resistance. A lamb was sacrificed and afterwards eaten at the

meal of the Jews' Pasch. The Lord warned the Jews in Egyptian bondage to sprinkle the door posts of their houses with the blood of a lamb. This would be a sign for the destroying angel to spare that house (Exodus 12).

On account of the purity (the wool) and meekness of the lamb and also on account of its sacrificial purpose, Christ is most aptly the Lamb of God. "He was offered because it was his own will, and he opened not his mouth. He shall be led as a sheep to the slaughter, and shall be dumb as a lamb before his shearer, and he shall not open his mouth" (Isaias 53:7). St. Peter tells his people that they have been bought "with the precious blood of Christ, as of a lamb unspotted and undefiled" (1 Peter 1:19).

St. John, the beloved Apostle, frequently in his Apocalypse designates the Redeemer as the Lamb. "And I saw, and beheld in the midst of the throne and of the four living creatures, a Lamb standing, as it were slain" (5). As in the Old Testament the Lamb was sacrificed for the remission of sins, so now in the New Testament, Christ is sacrificed for the sins of the world.

We pray in the *Agnus Dei,* twice, "have mercy on us." The priest (and people) strike their breast at these words to express the feelings of sinfulness and contrition of heart. They do desire so earnestly forgiveness. They beg Christ to be merciful to them and to pardon them their numerous sins. They are soon to receive Him in Communion and they wish to welcome Him with a clean soul and heart.

In the third *Agnus Dei,* the celebrant prays "grant us Thy peace." He begs Christ to give him this peace in Communion. How frequently the prayers are for peace! It is so necessary. We have peace when our soul is in order; when we place first things first and things unimportant last. When we have peace, our conscience is at ease and we are joyful. There are no storms of disturbed passions and desires.

In Requiem Masses, the prayer is "grant them rest"; and the priest does not strike his breast. At these Masses, we are more concerned with the departed. We beg God's mercy more toward them than toward us. We ask God to grant them eternal rest—liberation from Purgatory's suffering and entrance into Heaven's joyful rest.

Before the Communion of the people, the priest turns toward them after the Confiteor and holding a Particle over the Ciborium says aloud, "Behold the Lamb of God: Behold Him who taketh away the sins of the world!" Then follows thrice the "Lord, I am not worthy, etc." This is a call for the communicants to sincere contrition and a realization of their need. It is an act of faith in the Eucharist and His Redemption.

PRAYER OF PEACE

We are preparing for Holy Communion. Three most beautiful prayers serve as an immediate preparation. Never fail to say these prayers. They are found in your prayers for Mass at this place.

The first prayer is for peace. We have been begging for peace most urgently since the *Consecration*. We begged for peace in the third *Agnus Dei*. Now the priest develops and expands this petition. With his eyes on the Host, for he addresses Christ, the celebrant prays:

"O Lord Jesus Christ, Who said to Thy Apostles: Peace I leave with you, my peace I give unto you, regard not my sins but the faith of Thy Church, and deign to keep it in peace and unity, according to Thy will."

This prayer is suggested by the Redeemer's most tender discourse to His Apostles at the Last Supper (John 14:27). We have peace when our heart is not troubled nor afraid. The peace of Christ brings with it friendship with God, tranquillity of mind, calmness in trouble, joy in suffering, confidence in temptation. When we have the peace of Christ, we need not worry and weep as one that has no hope. We have peace with Christ and God when there is no quarrel, no dislike, no disobedience between us two. We are not at peace with God when we are in the friendship and obedience of His enemy, the devil. At this time, we are reminded of St. Theresa's prayer:

Let nothing trouble thee
Let nothing frighten thee
All things pass away
God alone suffices.

We pray for peace and unity in the Church. Humbly we pray Christ to disregard our sins, our disloyalty; to regard the faith and obedience of His Bride, the Church. Christ should protect the Church members for the sake of the elect—the heroism of martyrs, the purity of virgins, the justice of the good. We sinners should be chastised—rightly do we suffer—but spare us, O Lord, on account of the prayers of the saints.

How needy and poor we are at present! We are utterly helpless! The world is in a storm. Brother is against brother; Christian against Christian. Wars and rumors of wars. Grant us peace and unity, O Prince of Peace! "With humility and mildness, with patience support one another in charity, being careful to keep the unity of the Spirit in the bond of peace" (Ephesians 4:2). Through Christ we have peace, "making peace through the blood of His Cross, both as to the things that are on earth, and the things that are in heaven" (Colossians 1:20).

After this admirable prayer, at Solemn Mass the celebrant gives the kiss of peace to the deacon and sub-deacon. The sub-deacon gives it to the other clergy present. It is not now the kiss of the lips but a kind of embrace. The kiss is the customary expression of love, of friendship, of forgiveness. There are traitor's kisses also that are a mockery of what a kiss is to signify: the Judas kiss, the kiss of sinful pleasure and lustful passion.

The kiss of peace is most appropriate at this time of the Mass. We are going to receive Our Lord in Communion. To receive worthily we must be in His friendship. To be in His friendship, we must be at peace with our neighbor. The kiss of peace is a sign that we are at peace, that we have pardoned our neighbor. "Go first to be reconciled to thy brother, and then coming thou shalt offer thy gift" (Matthew 5:23). Charity to all—God and man—brings peace and unity. Hatred and pride beget quarrels and strife.

At Requiem Masses, this kiss of peace is not given, for the Sacrifice is then offered especially for the peace of the dead and not so much for the living. The kiss expresses joy and at Requiems we are mourning for the departed. On Holy Thursday it is also omitted to express the grief and sorrow of the Church at the treacherous kiss of Judas.

Questions for Discussion

1. Who is the Lamb of God and why?
2. Explain the ceremonies accompanying this prayer.
3. Explain "grant us peace".

PRAYERS BEFORE COMMUNION

Be sure to read this most beautiful second prayer before Communion:

> "O Lord, Jesus Christ, Son of the Living God, Who, according to the will of Thy Father, with the cooperation of the Holy Ghost, hast by Thy death given life to the world; deliver me by Thy most holy Body and Blood from all iniquities and from all evils; and make me always cleave to Thy commandments, and suffer me never to be separated from Thee, Who livest and reignest, etc."

With St. Peter, we profess faith in Christ Whom we are to receive. "Thou art Christ the Son of the living God" (Matt. 16:16). "I do believe, O Lord: help my unbelief" (Mark 9:23).

By the death of the Savior we have been given supernatural, everlasting life. "Who His own self bore our sins in His body upon the tree: that we, being dead to sins, should live to justice" (1 Peter 2:24). "We glory in the cross of Christ: in whom is our salvation, life and resurrection" (Galatians 6). "For as often as you shall eat this bread and drink the chalice, you shall show the death of the Lord until He come" (1 Cor. 11:26).

We pray to be delivered from all evils—spiritual and bodily. We may have in mind bodily health, temptations, worries, poverty, etc. Make me always obedient to Thy commandments as you were obedient to the Father! "He became obedient, obedient even unto the death of the Cross" (Philippians 2:8). "If thou wilt enter into Life, keep the commandments" (Matt. 19:17).

How tender and simple—childlike—is this petition, "do not permit me to be separated from Thee"! If we are always with Christ, we have nothing to fear. He never divorces us; we divorce Him and unite ourself with Satan. We are reminded of the two disciples at Emmaus, "Stay with us, because it is towards evening, and the day is now far spent. And He went in with them" (Luke 24:29). The Risen Christ after walking with them made as though he would leave them. This is a prayer we ought never forget. Say it very often. St. Philip Neri used to say, "Keep me, Lord, today, else I shall betray Thee."

The Third Prayer

The third and last prayer speaks of humility and confidence:

> Let not the partaking of Thy Body, O Lord Jesus Christ, which I, though unworthy, presume to receive, turn to my judgment and condemnation; but let it, through Thy mercy, become a safe-guard and remedy, both for soul and body.

The priest and the communicant remember the warning of St. Paul, "But let a man prove himself, and so let him eat of the bread and drink of the chalice. He that eateth and drinketh unworthily, eateth and drinketh judgment to himself" (1 Cor. 11:27, 28).

This cry of unworthiness is repeated thrice in the "Lord, I am not worthy that Thou shouldst enter under my roof", which is soon said. But Christ invites us to the Banquet, "Come to me, all you that labor and are burdened, and I will refresh you" (Matt. 11:28). Read the unparalleled thoughts for Mass and Communion in the *Imitation of Christ,* book IV. "It is out of grace and favor that thou art permitted to come to my table, as a beggar to a rich man's table, and he had no other return to make to him but to humble himself and give thanks" (Chap. XII).

Questions for Discussion

1. Explain the general idea of these three prayers, phrase by phrase.
2. Why do the Church and people pray so often for peace during Mass?
3. What is the best cure for worry and fear and scruple? Why?
4. Should Catholics be most joyful people? Why?
5. Read and explain the Introits for the Joy Sundays ("Laetare" and "Gaudete") the fourth Sunday in Lent and the third in Advent.
6. What is the "Kiss of Peace"?
7. What references are made to charity in these prayers and why?
8. What is the best preparation for Communion we can make?
9. Explain the *Domine Non Sum Dignus*.

THE COMMUNION

When the priest has concluded the triple "Lord, I am not worthy, etc." He takes the two sections of the Host into his right hand. He then makes the sign of the cross with them saying, "May the body of Our Lord Jesus Christ guard my soul unto eternal life. Amen." Thereupon he receives His Lord and Master in Communion. About a half minute is spent in contemplation of this mystery.

He uncovers the chalice and genuflects; with the paten he gathers whatever particles from the Host may have unavoidably fallen on the corporal (the white square cloth), and drops them into the chalice. During this action the celebrant prays

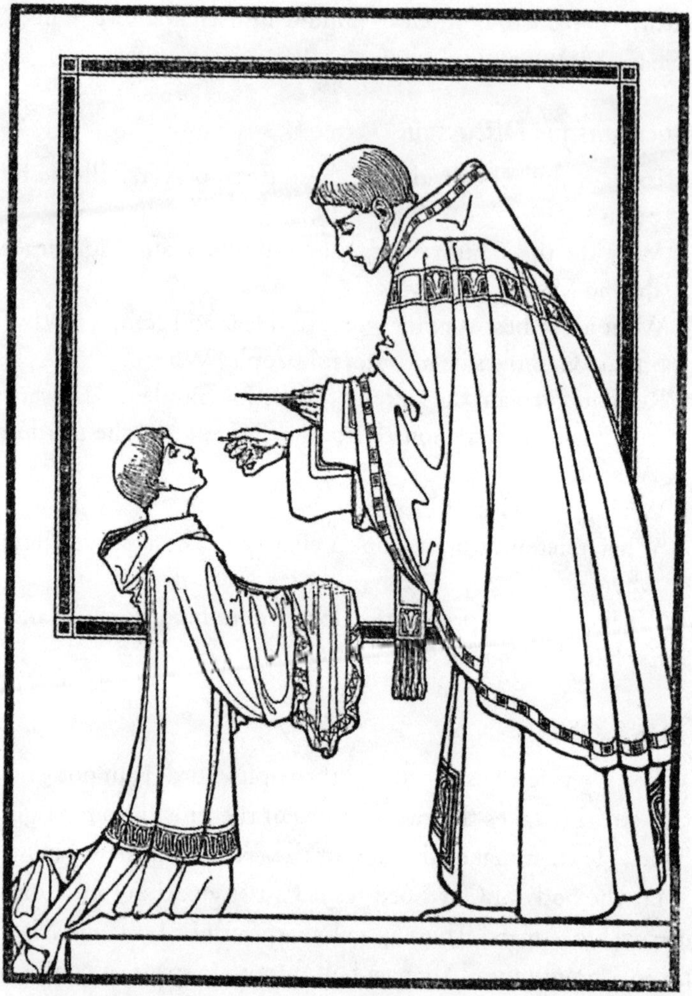

from the Psalms, "What shall I render to the Lord, for all the things that He hath rendered to me? I will take the chalice of salvation and I will call upon the name of the Lord. Praising I will call upon the Lord and I shall be saved from my enemies" (Psalm 115:12; Psalm 17:4). How can we thank God for His countless gifts? All He expects of us in return by way of appreciation and thanks is that we use them correctly—for His honor and glory. Indeed, we thank God most properly by taking more. The priest, after having received the greatest gift—the reception of sanctifying grace through the Most Holy Eucharist—then takes the chalice to double the gift, to receive more. Our God is so generous, so bountiful, that the way He wishes us to express thanks—so the Church says through her rubrics—is to accept more of His gifts that He so deeply wishes to give us.

Now making a sign of the cross with the chalice, the priest says, "May the blood of the Lord Jesus Christ guard my soul unto eternal life." He reverently receives the Precious Blood.

At this time the people approach the Holy Table for their Communion, their Banquet, the Bread of Angels. "The chalice of benediction, which we bless is it not the communion of the blood of Christ? And the bread, which we break, is it not the partaking of the body of the Lord" (1 Cor. 10:16). "As I live by the Father, so he that eateth me, the same shall live by me" (John 6:57).

The *Communion* is the return-gift of the Father. During the *Consecration* and *Offertory*, we give ourselves through Christ to God. Now the Father returns our Gift to be our best Food. In many sacrifices, the offerers ate of the victim in order to express their desire to share in the divinity. In our Communion we actually feed on God.

The Communion means taking complete part in the sacrifice. One should, if possible, receive daily and receive during Mass, not outside it. The order and sequence of the sacrifice is intentionally arranged so that the best reception of Communion occurs within the framework of the Holy Mass. Always receive at Mass, at least spiritually, if not sacramentally. An act of spiritual communion is made by warmly desiring Jesus to come to you. You will find such a prayer in your prayer book.

The best preparation and thanksgiving for Communion is the Mass. Say the Mass prayers. Unite yourself with Christ as Priest and Victim and love Him all your heart, all your soul, all your mind, and all your strength. We have considered the prayers of the Mass and have seen how wonderful they are. No better preparation for Communion in the way of prayers can be found than the *Confiteor*, the *Our Father*, the *Agnus Dei*, the *Lord I am not worthy*. The three prayers right before Communion are excellent. "As many as partake of the most holy Body and Blood of Thy Son at this altar, may be filled with every heavenly grace and blessing."

Upon receiving the Lord, whether sacramentally or spiritually, commune with Him, converse with Him, and let Him speak to you in silence, soul to soul, through the graces of the Blessed Sacrament.

Questions for Discussion

1. What is the best way of thanking God for His innumerable favors?
2. Why should one receive Communion at every Mass?
3. Why should one receive during Mass if possible, and not before or after Mass?
4. What is the best preparation for Communion?
5. How does Holy Communion worthily received make for charity among peoples?
6. Read Ellard, "The New Liturgy" in *The Catholic Mind* Feb. 22, 1937. p. 72. Also *Orate Fratres*, June 13, 1937, 31.

AFTER THE COMMUNION

The Purification

After his Communion, the priest offers the chalice to the server, who pours into it only wine. With the wine he rinses the chalice and then consumes it while saying, "What we have taken with our mouth, O Lord, may we receive with a pure mind; and from a temporal gift may it become for us an everlasting remedy."

Then the priest walks over to the server who pours into the chalice, over the priest's thumb and index-finger, both water and wine. He returns to the center and dries with the purificator these two digits. Meanwhile he says, "May Thy body, O Lord, which I have received and Thy blood, which I have drunk, adhere to my bowels, and grant that there may remain no stain of wickedness in me, whom the pure and holy sacraments have nourished."

We pray that His body and Blood may cleave to our soul, our hearts. In biblical language, the bowels are described as the seat, or organ, of the feelings and emotions, even of the will itself. St. Paul writes to the Philippians, "I long after you all in the bowels of Christ" (Phil. 1:8). We ask that the sacramental power and effects may remain in the faculties of the soul—will, memory, understanding. What better prayers can one find for a thanksgiving?

This is the purification: the priest rinses and dries the chalice, purifies it, so that no drops of Blood nor particles of the Host may remain in it. He also washes and dries his thumb and first-finger—with these he touched the Host—so that all particles might be removed, should there be any.

THE COMMUNION VERSE AND POSTCOMMUNION PRAYER

Now the priest goes to the Missal and reads the Communion antiphon. It was sung by the chanters during the distribution of Communion, as the offertory antiphon was sung during the collecting of the gifts. It is usually taken from a psalm or an epistle—some few have been composed by the Church or taken from the Saint's life—and touches upon a theme of the Mass that is pertinent to our reception of Holy Communion. Here is one for St. Augustine of Antioch (Feb. 1st), "I am the wheat of Christ; may I be ground by the teeth of the beasts that I be found a clean bread." The Communion verse allows us a short piece to meditate upon for our conversation with Christ in the reception of Holy Communion.

After the *Dominus Vobiscum* (The Lord be with you), the priest returns to the right side to read the *Post-Communion*. This is a prayer of thanksgiving after Communion and refers, as a rule, to the reception of the Eucharist as the *Secret* alludes to the giving of sacrificial gifts. These prayers are most remarkable. Always read and pray them well. We should all pray them, as they are prayers of petition asking for some good outcome from our participating in the Eucharistic Feast. Here are some examples: "Pour forth upon us the spirit of Thy charity, O Lord, that in Thy goodness Thou mayest make us of one mind and heart, etc" (Easter). "May the effect of Thy Sacrament possess our minds and bodies, so that Thy grace and not our emotions, may rule over us" (15th Sunday after Pentecost). "May we experience strength in mind and body, that healed in both, we may give glory, etc." (11th after Pentecost). "That we may be made worthy of Thy sacred Gifts make us ever obedient to Thy Commandments" (20th after Pentecost).

On week-days of Lent another prayer is said, the *Prayer over the people*. It was meant to ask God's blessing especially for those who had not received Holy Communion, lest they be deprived of a prayer. A much more likely explanation may be found in the fact that this prayer is invariably the prayer for Vespers. In Lent, centuries ago, Vespers was said after Mass immediately before the dismissal of the people as is still the case in the Mass and shortened Vespers on Holy Saturday. In Lent now, we have only at Mass the prayer and not the Psalms and Magnificat of Vespers.

Questions for Discussion

1. What prayers should be said after receiving Communion—should one neglect to follow the Missal?
2. Should one leave the Church immediately after Mass when one has received? How long should the communicant be engaged in thanksgiving?
3. What is the spirit of the *Postcommunion?*
4. What is the "Prayer over the People"?

THE BLESSING AND DISMISSAL

After the last prayer, the priest wishes the people, "May the Lord be with you." Now as you return to your daily work, may the Lord accompany you. May He be with you in your sorrows and joys as a comfort and as a friend. Then he dismisses them in the words, "Ite, missa est" (Go, the Mass is said. It is in the dismissal). From these relatively unimportant words, "missa" arose: the name for the complete action of the sacrifice—Mass. In the first centuries, the Sacrifice of the Mass was called the Mystery or the Breaking of Bread; not the Mass as now. The word "Mass" comes, it is said, from "missa" (dismissal) of the *Ite, missa est.*

At Masses when there is no *Gloria,* (the times of penance and sorrow), there is said, "Benedicamus Domino" (Let us bless the Lord). These words were used to have the people stay after Mass for more services. At Requiems, "May they rest in peace" is said: a last request for the dead is expressed.

Since the 12th century, the formal dismissal of the people no longer marks the conclusion of the Mass. Only at Masses of bishops was a blessing given formerly to the worshippers. Gradually, the priest, about to leave the altar, began to bless the people. Now the blessing is the rule, except at Requiems when we attend to the dead primarily.

> May the tribute of my worship be pleasing to Thee, O Holy Trinity; and grant that the Sacrifice which I, though unworthy, have offered up to the sight of Thy Majesty, may be acceptable to Thee, and through Thy mercy may be a propitiation for me, and all those for whom I have offered it. Through Christ Our Lord. Amen.

The priest (and people) expressed the dispositions which have animated him during the Holy Sacrifice. He repeats the reasons for sacrifice. This prayer was at first part of the priest's private thanksgiving. It was made part of the Mass, with the *Blessing* and *Last Gospel,* in the 16th century.

The Blessing is now given in the words, "May God Almighty bless you: the Father, the Son and the Holy Ghost." It is a last request that we profit from the Mass; that we realize the value of the Mass; that we appreciate it. It is a very special blessing. It is the continued application of the Cross. All graces and blessings have their source in the Cross. How we should love the blessing of God's minister! Read the admirable words said by the bishop at the consecrating of the priest's hands during Holy Orders: "O God, consecrate and sanctify these hands, through our unction and Thy blessing, that whatsoever things they shall bless, may be blessed: and whatsoever things they may consecrate, may be consecrated and made holy in the name of Our Lord Jesus Christ." Ask often for the blessing of Christ's deputy, the priest.

Questions for Discussion

1. What is the origin of the word "Mass"?
2. Explain the summarizing prayer said before the Blessing?
3. Why is the Blessing omitted in some Masses?

THE LAST GOSPEL

What a grand ending for the Mass! The first fourteen verses of chapter one of the Gospel of St. John is a fitting close to the Mystery of Faith. In these few verses we have a summary, a synopsis, of the whole of revelation, of our religion. It speaks of the Trinity, creation, Incarnation, our spiritual adoption as sons of God by grace. In other words, it is the history of the Mass! St. Augustine says these fourteen verses of St. John should be "written in letters of gold and set up in all the churches in a prominent place" (*City of God* X, 29). The more one reads this chapter, the more will he appreciate it and see how it tells of God's love for us. Our "thanks be to God" at the end of it will be sincere, attentive and especially heartfelt. It will be a little thanks for our great gift of the Gospel and of the Mass.

At times, when on the same day two very important feasts fall, the *Last Gospel* gives way to the Gospel of the feast commemorated.

This *Last Gospel* was added to the Mass by Pope Pius V (1570). Originally it was part of the priest's private thanksgiving and was said by him on his way to the sacristy. The Gospel of St. John, and especially this section, was—and still is—held in great respect by the people. They considered it a great spiritual and bodily help to have it read over them. It is used especially in prayers and blessings for the sick, particularly children. There are small papers on which it is printed and these (wrapped in cloth) are worn by the sick. Probably this Gospel chapter was placed in the Mass so that all the people could have it read over them—so numerous were the requests to have it read for their spiritual and temporal benefit.

Questions for Discussion

1. Why does this *Last Gospel* form a fitting ending for the Mass?
2. Explain the *Last Gospel*?
3. What is meant by the sacramental, "St. John's Gospel"?
4. For an explanation of the vestments and sacred vessels read Gihr's *The Sacrifice of the Mass*.

SUMMARY

A REVIEW OF SACRIFICE

We have considered the prayers and the ceremonies of the Mass. Now, let us repeat a few of the essentials of the Mass. These must never be forgotten, and must always be present in mind at our attendance at the Holy Sacrifice.

The Mass is the sacrifice of Christ; it is the continued renewal of Calvary; it is making Christ present as victim, the Lamb of God. It is the distribution of the graces the Redeemer won for us on Calvary. On the Cross, Christ offered Himself to His Heavenly Father in a bloody manner; here, on the altar, He renews that offering in an unbloody manner. How? In the very fact that He becomes present at the Consecration, He becomes present as the Victim slain and offered on Calvary: He (Christ) thereby expresses His acts and words of atonement, obedience, resignations, love, sorrow for our sins, etc. God sees under the veil of bread and wine the death of Christ; sees Christ the Victim, the Lamb of God, and accepts the Son's prayers and acts of repentance, adoration, praise, thanks, etc., in behalf of the people. Christ, if we ask Him, speaks for us.

The word "sacrifice" usually confuses us; it seems hard to grasp and understand. Let us think of it simply as a gift to God to show our sorrow, thanks, praise, need and adoration. Sacrifice is a token-payment to God of our debt to Him. Parents give gifts to the children, and children give gifts of some sort to their parents. Friends give presents to friends; lovers to their sweethearts. We send flowers, candy, books, jewelry, etc., on birthdays, deaths, weddings. Why? "Actions speak louder than words." Gifts, externally given and received, represent, express the interior feelings and sentiments. Gifts are symbols of love, sorrow, thanks, etc. They are the spokesmen of the heart and soul.

In St. Matthew's Gospel (2:11), the three wise men from the East "found the Child with Mary his Mother, and falling down they adored Him; and opening their treasures, they offered him gifts: gold, frankincense and myrrh." The gifts spoke the faith, adoration, thanks, humility, etc., of the Three Kings.

We owe a fourfold debt to God as our Creator, Sanctifier, Protector, Reward—our Highest Good. It is a debt of sorrow, thanks, petition and adoration. We can begin to pay this debt with prayers and a good life. With a gift, the Sacrifice of the Mass, of Christ, we can make fitting payment. In the Mass we ask God to accept the payment of His Son in whom the Father was well pleased. In attending and following the Mass, we ask Christ, present as a Sacrifice on the altar, to pay our debts to God, the Father. And He does. Read here St. Paul's Letter to the Hebrews, chapters 8–11; also read your Mass prayers for after the Consecration.

A REVIEW OF THE OFFERTORY

Our gift to God is made through bread and wine which become the Body and Blood of Christ. Bread and wine are the most fitting externals of our offerings. Why? Because bread and wine are most close to life, are necessary for life. We should give our life, our blood to God, for it belongs to Him, we are His creatures. But God does not expect our blood so we give to Him what keeps and supports life: food. And the staple and usual food at the time of Christ (and still in many lands) is bread and wine. Abraham was about to slay Isaac, his son; and the Lord forbade him, "Lay not thy hand on the boy; now I know that thou fearest God and sparest not thy only begotten son for my sake" (Genesis 22:12).

Bread and wine not only symbolize our life, but also our toil, our labors, difficulties and sorrows. These we dedicate to God, and endure willingly as His creatures. "In the sweat of thy brow thou shalt earn thy bread."

We have bread and wine as the elements of our Sacrifice for they express so well the unity and charity that should prevail among Christians. As the bread is made from many grains of wheat, and the wine from many grapes, so we being many are one body, one Church, one Christ. "And the bread, which we break, is it not the partaking of the body of the Lord? For we being many, are one bread, one body, all that partake of one bread" (1 Cor. 10:16–17).

Since we are one in Christ—represented in the bread and wine and realized in the Eucharist—we must be charitable to one another. This fact the early Christians lived so excellently that it was one great cause of the rapid growth of the Church. "And the multitude of believers had but one heart and one soul: . . . neither was there any one needy among them" (Acts 4:32–34). As the bread and wine become good food only by milling and crushing and baking, so we become fit for God and society only by crushing and pressing of ill-will and evil ways.

If our gift is to be acceptable to God it must be true and sincere. God is not deceived. When we tell Him, through our gift, we are repentant; that we worship Him, etc., we must mean it; otherwise, our gift is worthless, practically. Our Lord warns us, "If, therefore, thou offer thy gift at the altar, and there thou remember that thy brother hath anything against thee; leave there thy offering, and go first to be reconciled to thy brother, and then coming thou shalt offer thy gift" (Matt. 5:23–24). At the offertory of the Mass, we pray, "In a spirit of humility and contrition of heart may we be received by Thee, etc." Our benefits from the Mass are in proportion to our contrition, devotion and sincerity.

Cain and Abel offered sacrifices. Cain offered the poorest; Abel, the best. God was pleased at Abel's gift, and the Church includes his name in her holy Canon. With Cain's gifts God was displeased and Cain became jealous. Let us offer our gifts generously and with sincerity. "The gift without the giver is bare."

At the Offertory on Sundays, we usually make a coin offering. Let this be generous and representative. This expresses our sacrifice, our giving of self, our dependence on God.

A Review of the Consecration

At the *Offertory* of the Mass we get our gifts of bread and wine ready. We separate them from the world and we bless them. We dedicate them to God in two beautiful prayers:

> "Receive, O Lord, this unspotted host, which I Thy unworthy servant offer to Thee, for my sins . . . for all faithful Christians, living and dead, that it may avail unto salvation."

And at the chalice:

> "We offer Thee the chalice of salvation beseeching Thy clemency that it may ascend as a sweet odor for our salvation, etc."

At the *Offertory*, through the bread and wine, we ask God to accept us with our joys and sorrows. To make our consecration of self to God more meaningful, we give a gift in money to the church. This money offering symbolizes our paying of debts due to God and giving our material contribution to the sacrifice at hand.

At the *Consecration* our bread and wine become the body and blood of Christ, the Lamb of God. Only the externals, the appearances of bread and wine remain; their substance—what makes them bread and wine—is changed. Now our gift, our Sacrifice, is the Son of God. That is why the Mass is the greatest, the best possible Sacrifice: it is that of His only-begotten Son in whom the Father is well pleased. "What things are pleasing to Him [the Father] I do always." We know the Father received this Sacrifice of the Son (and of us) for He gave His approval in the Resurrection and Ascension of Jesus.

Christ is on our altar after the *Consecration*. He is there interceding for us. And this is the time to say the prayers to be found in the prayerbooks or Missal: "Vouchsafe, O Lord, to accept our Gifts as Thou wast pleased to accept the offering of Thy servants Abel, Abraham and Melchisedech." "We humbly beseech Thee to command that these our offerings be borne by the hands of Thy holy angel to Thine altar on high, etc."

We have already said Christ is on our altar as He was on the Cross only in a different manner (unbloody and invisible). He is on the altar as a Victim, the Lamb of God, and Priest. Offer Him to the Father; The Father accepts Him and us too if we unite ourselves as victims to Him. The Father sees us in and with the Son and the Father accepts us and our pledges and promises of praise, thanks, sorrows, etc. "Be mindful, O Lord, of Thy servants . . . who now pay their vows to Thee."

What power and strength we have at Mass! We are not alone; we are not helpless. We are with Christ; He is with us and praying with us; our strength is the strength of Christ. Say your prayers of the Mass during Mass and you will be sure you are offering a pleasing sacrifice to God. St. Bonaventure says, "First of all God sends His Son down to us upon the altar, then the Church [we] sends Him back to the Father, to make intercession for us." "Through Him and with Him and in Him is to Thee, God the Father in unity with the Holy Ghost, all honor and glory."

A Review of the Communion

At the *Communion*, the Father returns the Gift which earlier in the Mass we offered him. At the *Consecration* we gave to God; now He gives to us. God is not outdone in generosity—when we give to Him, He returns to us hundredfold.

At Holy Communion we partake of the Victim, Christ. In some ancient sacrifices, the Jews were commanded to eat of the gifts sacrificed. They realized the sacrificed lamb or fruits were in a very special manner holy and sanctified. They ate of it to become sanctified. In Holy Communion we eat the body and blood of Christ to become more and more sharers in the holiness of Christ.

Recall again some beautiful prayers before *Communion*, "Lamb of God, Who takest away the sins of the world, have mercy on us!" "Lord, I am not worthy that Thou shouldst enter under my roof, etc." And this prayer of prayers, "Deliver me by this most sacred body and blood from all evils; make me always adhere to Thy commandments, and never allow me to be separated from Thee." All the prayers immediately before *Communion* serve as a preparation. Say them earnestly and contritely—as one really needing help.

Also realize that at every Mass we should try to receive. The Communion gives a certain fullness and completeness to the Mass. Christ wants to be received as well as offered. Allow Him to help you in every good way.

Always realize the Mass is your Sacrifice and not the priest's alone. Offer the Mass to God with the priest; say the prayers of the Mass. The people are not simply spectators at this Sacrifice; they do not come only to *hear* Mass. The expression of "hearing" Mass is unfortunate—we come to pray the Mass and offer ourselves in it, not simply hear the words spoken and see the actions done. The people come to take part in this greatest of Sacrifices. Therefore, follow the Mass not only in spirit but in prayer as well—read the prayers of the Mass. Come not to hear and see this Great Action, the Drama of Calvary, but to take part in it—to offer and to receive the Victim, the Hero.

It Is the Mass That Matters

> "The Mass is a mystery so tremendous, so profoundly attractive, so intimately associated with the keystone of the Christian faith, so vouched for by the testimony of Saints . . . If the Incarnation is indeed the one divine event to which the whole creation moves, the miracle of the altar may well seem its restful shadow cast over a dry and thirsty land, for the help of man who is apt to be discouraged if perpetually told that everything really important and interesting happened once for all,

long ago, in chill, historic past. It is the Mass that matters. It is the Mass that makes the difference, so hard to define—so subtle is it, yet so perceptible—between a Catholic country and a Protestant one, between Dublin and Edinburgh, between Havre and Cromer" (Augustin Birrell, (non-Catholic) in *The Nineteenth Century*, April, 1896).

AN EXHORTATION

In his exhortation to the new priests, the ordaining bishop during the sacrament of Holy Orders, speaks these awful words to the candidates, "Realize what you do; imitate what you enact."

We may call these words the keynote, the theme, of the priest's life. His life is to be lived in the light of these all-inclusive words. And they apply very especially to the people also. They as Christians, as members of the Mystical Body of Christ, are to "realize what they do" at Mass and to "imitate what they enact" in the offering of their prayers in union with the Sacrifice. Appreciate the Mass. Recognize what is going on at the altar. You are on Calvary. The Cross is brought into the present, into today. The death of the Savior is being represented. He dies sacramentally. Christ is born again and dies again. "Jesus Christ yesterday, today and the same forever."

"Imitate what you handle [treat, enact]." In other words, you are to be victims with Christ. "Go and do likewise!" Upon the paten and in the chalice is our flesh and blood. We are "living sacrifices" (Rom. 12:1). It is not bread and wine which we offer to God—it is our complete life with and through and in Christ. Christ died, suffered, and endured all things in sacrifice. A victim must be changed by being broken. So must we break our evil tendencies, habits; break our bad will. You are not only priests but also victims. The gifts of bread and wine stand for your life. It is a complete offering, a holocaust offering, an offering of our entire selves. To be a victim with Christ is to have His sentiments, dispositions, His virtues of obedience, patience, resignation, etc.

"I beseech you, brethren, by the mercy of God, that you present your bodies a living sacrifice, holy, pleasing unto God, your reasonable service. And be not conformed to this world: but be reformed in the newness of your mind, that you may prove what is the good, and the acceptable and the perfect will of God" (Rom. 12:1).

"He doth not know Thee, O Jesus Christ, who dishonoreth even Thy shadow. I honor all things where I find the intention of honoring Thee . . . The censer which waves round the priest; the Gloria sung in choir; the peaceful light of the perpetual lamp; these lighted tapers—all is done for Thee. Why is the Host elevated if it be not to honor Thee, O Jesus Christ, Who are dead for love of us? Because it is no more, and Thou art It, the believing Church bends the knee . . . The riches collected from distant countries, the magnificence of chasubles—all that has relation to Thee." (Lavater, *The Veiled Majesty*, p. 303).

Questions for Discussion

1. Give a summary of the spirit, idea and purpose of sacrifice.
2. Explain the meaning and thought of the *Offertory*, the *Consecration*, the *Communion*.
3. Read "THE LITURGY and LEAKAGE" in the *Catholic Digest*, July, 1937, p. 71.

"Now to the king of ages, immortal, invisible, the only God, be honor and glory for ever and ever. Amen" (1 Timothy 1:17).